TOWARDS MY NEIGHBOUR

TOWARDS
MY NEIGHBOUR

The Social Influence of
the Rotary Club Movement in
Great Britain and Ireland

by

C. R. HEWITT

LONGMANS, GREEN AND CO
LONDON · NEW YORK · TORONTO

LONGMANS, GREEN AND CO LTD
6 & 7 CLIFFORD STREET LONDON W I

ALSO AT MELBOURNE AND CAPE TOWN

LONGMANS, GREEN AND CO INC
55 FIFTH AVENUE NEW YORK 3

LONGMANS, GREEN AND CO
215 VICTORIA STREET TORONTO I

ORIENT LONGMANS LTD
BOMBAY CALCUTTA MADRAS

First published 1950

Printed in Great Britain by Richard Clay and Company, Ltd.,
Bungay, Suffolk

PREFACE

ONCE the governing body of *Rotary International in Great Britain and Ireland* had been authorized to proceed with a historical survey of their Association and its work, they faced the question whether it should be written by a Rotarian or by someone from outside the movement. They decided that it should be a non-Rotarian view; and they chose me. They gave me a free hand in critical appraisal—they would censor nothing, withhold no information, confine their surveillance to the assured correctness of facts. Whatever judgments may be passed upon the book that has resulted, no-one will dispute that this was a courageous and even daring step; and the book is in all respects the one I should have written even if it had not been at their behest that I undertook the work. I was to learn that it is typical of their attitude to criticism and their determination not to function as a secret society.

It sounded a comfortable assignment. True, as a non-Rotarian I knew little of their movement. I had been to one or two Rotary lunches. I knew from Press reports that their meetings were often chosen by leading publicists and even statesmen as occasions for important speeches. I had read some of the American authors who have singled them out for satire. I was indeed to find that in this country they afforded much the same scope for satire as any other exclusive association, since exclusiveness provokes angry conjecture among the excluded. But to write their story, even to write it objectively, must be a simple matter of research, selection, comparison, and presentment.

It was not. It entailed meeting hundreds of Rotarians, going to their conferences, assemblies, councils, and committee meetings, hearing the stored wisdom of one member refuted by the keener insight of another, watching and listening for half-heartedness or self-delusion, trying to assess motives—and from time to time inoculating oneself against a genuine and pervasive *bonhomie* that endangered the critical faculty. This last was among the more difficult feats, though it turned a research job into a happy adventure. Ulysses was not more beset by temptation.

But I would here record the opinion that, if this account had been written by some of the experienced Rotarians I met, it would be considerably more critical than it is. No outside critic has ever outdone the blistering witticisms and the scornful denigration with which these men upbraid the movement they all unaffectedly love. For the most part, they deplore that Rotary, in its desire to preserve unanimity in the Clubs and abstain from the approval or condemnation of other movements, will not express a ' corporate ' opinion upon any political or theological question. They are fairly evenly divided about this. The controversy will keep their Movement healthy for a long time to come. I have convinced myself, independently, that the Movement in its present form would not long survive a departure from this admittedly restrictive covenant.

The extent of its social services was a great surprise to me. I sought my information from over a hundred societies with whom it co-operates in this regard, obstinately taking nothing for granted that I learned from Rotary archives and literature—to which I was given absolute freedom of access. I have told the story as I thus learned it. It seems a very remarkable story to me.

C. R. Hewitt

CONTENTS

Chapter One

WHAT ROTARY IS

WHEREVER in this sociable world men meet periodically for coffee, beer, or food, you have a club. They do this in every town and village from Shanghai to San Francisco, and they have done it in every age since the agriculturist displaced the nomad; but they have not called themselves a ' club ' until their common interests suggested agreed rules of conduct. Thereupon they have often felt the need of a *rationale*, of some purpose beyond the social pleasures to be had in a ' sodality '. ' We now use the word club,' said John Aubrey in the seventeenth century, ' for a sodality in a tavern '; and Pepys recorded that he and his friends resorted for ' clubbing ' to a Westminster coffee-house called ' The Rota '.

The temptation to relate the modern Rotary Club to ' The Rota ' must be resisted; the evidence is lacking. Rotary Clubs, indeed, whose known origins will be discussed in a later chapter, owe nothing to their name and everything to the familiar desire for companionship, well-doing, and the manifest attractions of a co-operative rather than a competitive society. If we are to follow the history of the Rotary Movement in this country, we can hardly begin better, therefore, than by examining it as it is today, considering briefly what it does as compared with what it professes or hopes to do, whether its influence is vital or negligible, good or bad—and, above all, what it *is*.

*   *   *   *   *

Rotarians call themselves ' a world fellowship of business and professional men united in the ideal of service '. By ' service ' they must be understood to mean, not the after-sale maintenance of commodities that need expert attention to fulfil their purpose for a competitive period, but the abnegation of self. They hold before themselves the ideal of giving something for nothing; of giving to the public, that is to say, an undebited balance in the form of scrupulously fair dealing to customers, clients, suppliers, and employees, and to the world at large such benefit as they are specially able to confer through their status as important representatives of commerce and the professions. To what extent they are in fact 'representative' of their vocations will be discussed later. A vocation, they hold, is something more than a means to a livelihood: it is an opportunity to improve the common lot. 'Service in vocation through fellowship' is one of numerous phrases by which Rotarians, in an introspective literature that grows annually in volume, have sought to define their purpose. 'Service above self' is the one they have adopted as their motto. And there are many among them who strive with the deepest sincerity to fulfil it.

* * * * *

To follow their story, we must adopt some of their terminology. They call their movement 'Rotary'; and, as with many movements of united men, the adopted name has lost its original meaning and acquired a mysticism and a sanctity that seem incongruous to the onlooker able to recognize it only as a verbal convenience. When they say 'Rotary' to each other, they may be referring to Rotary International as a world organization, to the Rotary Clubs of Great Britain and Ireland as a semi-autonomous society within the International, to the declared objects of the Movement, to its frailties and failures and successes, or to the behaviour of its members. They sometimes personify Rotary and call it 'she'. They endow it with the corporate qualities commonly bestowed by the protesting or admiring individual upon the crowd. They tend to see it as a timeless force, with a capital 'R' and an existence of its own. They disapprove of it, defend it, criticize it, and love it.

How did it come by its name, which has for years been a source of unholy joy to its enemies? Rotarians know all the gibes about rotundity, passing the liquor round, rolling home, and the fatuous circularity of arriving repeatedly back at one's ideological starting-point. There are rival theories about the origin of the name, but there seems little doubt that Paul Harris, the Chicago lawyer who inspired the formation of the first of the Clubs in 1905, provided the reason by proposing that its members should meet at each other's business premises 'in rotation'.

At a third meeting of the Chicago group [wrote Harris in *My Road to Rotary*] I presented several suggestions as a name for the Club, among them 'Rotary'; and that name was selected, as we were then holding our meetings in rotation at our offices and places of business. Later, still rotating, we held our meetings at various hotels and restaurants. Thus we began as 'Rotarians', and such we continue to be.

Dr. Thomas Stephenson, honorary secretary in 1923 of the then British Association of Rotary Clubs, wrote in a pamphlet on *Rotary, Its History, Its Interpretation, and Its Possibilities* that Paul Harris ' saw the advantage of the close friendship produced and how the services rendered and the benefits conferred would go round the members—would " rotate ", in fact—and he called his circle the " Rotary Club ". That was the beginning of the Rotarian movement.' Other efforts have been made in recent years to justify the retention of the name in the absence of any rotatory movement of the Clubs (they now meet weekly, and in a very few cases fortnightly, at a fixed place). It has been related by some Rotarians to the principle—an unwritten and indeed a neglected one—that Club members must sit next to a different neighbour at every weekly lunch-meeting.

As an explanation of the name the latter theory is the least acceptable and is discountenanced by all Rotarians learned in their lore. Nor is Dr. Stephenson's given credence today; but it throws an interesting light on 'Rotary' as it was before it acquired the dynamic of an outward-looking crusade. In its early years it was openly and unashamedly an association of business men concerned to promote their personal interests, primarily their own, incidentally (and of course happily enough) those of their fellow-members.

*   *   *   *   *

It is an important, though frequently disregarded principle of the Movement that a man cannot apply to join a Rotary Club. He must wait until he is asked. A Rotary Club, as originally conceived, comprised one man from each of a carefully-compiled list of trades and professions in the locality which it served, and each of those vocations was called a ' classification '. A would-be Rotarian (there are many would-be Rotarians, and they are disappointed men) might one day be offered membership, but it would be because his ' classification ' in the Club that sought him out had fallen vacant or because a Club was being newly formed in his locality. And before he was approached, as we shall see later, he would have been the unsuspecting subject of searching enquiries as to what may conveniently be called his 'Rotary' qualities. The approach would not, at least in theory, be due to the fact that he wanted to join.

Membership of the Clubs was, moreover, confined to men in 'executive' positions—which included men running their own businesses. It is a *sine qua non* of the Movement that members must be in a position, as owners or managers or 'executives', to influence the conduct not merely of their own firms but also of their trades or callings as a collective whole. To this end they are repeatedly urged, indeed almost required, to join also their trade and professional associations. They are to carry the principles of 'Rotary', by example and to a lesser extent by precept, into their vocations; and they are to represent their vocations, for informative and 'educational' but *not* for profit-seeking purposes, within the Rotary Clubs themselves. The 'single classification' system provokes much criticism, on the ground that it excludes men who would make good members, a complaint which no Rotarian attempts to deny or refute. But every kind of club, it is pointed out, needs some method of discrimination to keep its membership within convenient numerical limits, and, for social reasons, most kinds of clubs must be composed of men who can mix together without financial embarrassments. Employees and workers in the humbler ranks of industry and the professions complain, often heatedly, that 'Rotary' is a snob organization of masters and bosses, serving class interests to the detriment of the poor and, for all they know, conspiring against them under the hypocritical banner of 'Service above self'. Rotarians are not deaf to this accusation; indeed, they include among their number a few who voice it themselves. In general, the answer is that 'Rotary', though in theory open to men of all creeds and classes, depends for the realization of its aims and objects on the membership of influential and representative men. This, therefore, will be a convenient moment to set out, in words chosen by the Movement itself but often criticized by Rotarians for their inadequacy, the *Objects of Rotary*.

    *   *   *   *   *

The *Objects of Rotary* are to encourage and foster the ideal of service as a basis of worthy enterprise and, in particular, to encourage and foster :

1. The development of acquaintance as an opportunity for service.
2. High ethical standards in business and professions; the recognition of the worthiness of all useful occupations; and the dignifying by each Rotarian of his occupation as an opportunity to serve society.
3. The application of the ideal of service by every Rotarian to his personal, business and community life.
4. The advancement of international understanding, goodwill and peace through a world fellowship of business and professional men united in the ideal of service.

These are recognized to be general principles. They attract accusations of 'woolliness' and of face-saving vagueness, not always from non-Rotarians. A more cogent criticism is, perhaps, that the Movement purports to leave its members free as individuals to interpret and apply these four cardinal principles in accordance with their own consciences, while it issues from headquarters such a flow of 'inspirational' literature as to invite comparison with a highly-literate evangelical society. It is considered that this policy is essential for the maintenance of a further principle, namely that

the general welfare of the community is of concern to the members of the club, and the merits of any public question involving such welfare may be fairly and intelligently studied and discussed at the meetings of the club for the enlightenment of its members in forming their individual opinions. *The club shall not, however, express an opinion on any pending controversial public measure.*[1]

The main concern of the Movement is with the individual, whose integrity is to be preserved at whatever cost in administrative difficulty. Rotarians see that this must prevent ' Rotary ' from ' having in any corporate sense the public force and estimation which it otherwise might easily possess '. In a headquarters pamphlet called *Synopsis of Rotary* appears this frank statement, typical of an appetite for self-criticism that is rare in associations whose literature is available for anyone to read :

The public understands and appreciates a movement which stands definitely and solidly for some specific line of action, and it is naturally

[1] The Standard Constitution for Rotary Clubs, Article IX (1).

apt to discount and to ignore one which, by setting itself to unite all men of goodwill and of good endeavour, thereby debars itself in the main from any corporate declaration other than one in favour of certain abstract principles of conduct. And the danger will always necessarily be, of course, one which is inherent in abstractions and generalizations : that they lack the touchstone of reality and of real trial, and are apt to provide a phylactery for the hypocrite and a cloak for the self-complacent.

None of ' Rotary's ' critics, of whom perhaps the bitterest have been Sinclair Lewis, H. L. Mencken, and G. K. Chesterton, has gone farther than that : they have been more abusive—we will consider later some of the things they have said—but less succinct; and because they have been more excited, they have been noticeably less fair.

The four ' Objects of Rotary ' were seen to provide scope for four kinds of committees; Rotarians have carried the fashion of committee-forming to what must be its ultimate degree, a fact which, in a society exalting the individual above the group, is one of their most paradoxical achievements. The first ' Object ' is the concern, in every Club, of a ' Club Service Committee ', which concerns itself with the smelling-out of likely new members and their instruction in the purposes of the Movement, with the admittedly sporadic enforcement of an extremely strict ' attendance rule ' (a member must attend, in each year, sixty per cent of the weekly lunches, or automatically cease to be a member), with the arrangement of social events and the procuring of lunch-time speakers, and with the promotion of ' fellowship ' within the Club. The second ' Object ' is furthered by a ' Vocational Service Committee ', which may be said to ' educate ' every Club member in the standard of conduct he is expected to observe in his business or profession. The third ' Object ' inspires a ' Community Service Committee ', whose main concern is the propagation of that good citizenship which leads individuals to associate themselves (outside the Club) with the ameliorative social services—cultural activities, hospital work, care of the blind, the deaf, and the bedridden, prison-visiting, slum clearance, boys' clubs and camps, and a host of similar good works. The fourth ' Object ' informs the work of an ' International Service Committee ' for the promotion of world peace and understanding, international fellowship through correspondence and personal

contacts with Rotarians in more than eighty other countries, and—
perhaps above all—the inculcation of the 'international outlook'
in the minds of young people. In this final respect a Rotary
Foundation, deploying considerable financial resources, operates
a soundly conceived and rapidly growing scheme for the interchange of graduates between the leading Universities of the
world, where they study the life and customs of countries to
which they are strangers and, as a condition of a generous
fellowship award, act as youthful ambassadors of goodwill.

These four committees have their counterparts in 'District'
Organizations, of which there are eighteen, each covering several
counties and in some cases as many as eighty Clubs. These
organizations are known as District Councils, and all their committees are reproduced yet again, on a more august level, in
'R.I.B.I.' (Rotary International in Great Britain and Ireland),
the central body in this country. It is typical of the way in
which Rotarians seek to preserve the international appearance
of their organization that all these committees are further represented in 'Rotary International', the Chicago-based parent of
'Rotary' throughout the world. It is often said, and not least by
Rotarians themselves, that in a movement essentially individualistic
this superstructure of committees resembles an inverted pyramid,
with the individual Club member at the apex. It will, indeed,
appear in the following pages that the system works, and that
supporting the inverted pyramid stand others the right way up,
with men of acknowledged leadership sending down instruction
to four-square formations of men ready for 'Service'.

* * * * *

Service to humanity is the Rotarian's ideal, though he frequently
differs from the hierarchy of the Movement as to the form which
it should take. Isolated acts of social compassion, the 'whip-
round' for the needy case brought to the Club's notice from
outside, have a perennial appeal to the individual Rotarian which
will always be proof against 'Rotary's' deprecating references to
'service at soup-kitchen level'. 'Rotary' holds, in its present
stage of ideological development, that the Movement should
either concern itself with the amelioration of wrongs which are
outside the scope of specialist organizations, or give such service
as it can to such organizations as exist. Rotarians, on the other

hand, tend to hold that if they see a job to be done that they can do, then if it redounds to someone's relief or greater happiness they can do it whether ' Rotary ' approves or not.

The antithesis, as between ' Rotary ' and Rotarians, will be found to proclaim itself repeatedly as the story of Rotary Clubs is followed, and it represents what are in essence the growing-pains of a great Movement; a Movement which is even now in process of forming an ethos, and follows the pattern of its countless predecessors and contemporaries, religious, lay, and pagan, in pursuing the Good by the road of the extrovert. It was not always so. In its early years ' Rotary ' was a loosely knit association of Clubs in which, after a good weekly lunch and much conviviality, members stood up and testified to the increased business their membership had brought them. They named the fellow-Rotarian to whom they had sold this or from whom they had bought that. They filled in forms which showed what business had been transacted as a consequence of membership, and from these forms there were compiled periodical returns showing what ' Rotary ' had done for its members. There was no pretence whatsoever that improved business was not an important reason for the Club's existence; and while there was no pretence, the critics of Rotary Clubs were few.

*　　*　　*　　*　　*

But then Rotarians, dissatisfied with a coldly materialistic basis to their ' Fellowship ', decided that they must express an ethic and go in for good works. They decided, in fact, that ' he profits most who serves best ',[1] and service became their avowed motive. Within a very short time they became the target of the most vitriolic criticism from publicists of various kinds, mainly American. Ethics? Service? They were business men, were they not? And among those writers who always feel it to be their duty to detect and castigate hypocrisy there were many who proceeded to profit most by serving their least charitable readers best. We shall see what application those criticisms have to organized ' Rotary ' today.

---

[1] A slogan first suggested by Arthur F. Sheldon, editor of a Chicago journal called *The Business Philosopher*, and adopted in 1909 as the official motto of Rotary International. It was never adopted by ' R.I.B.I.', which officially discountenanced it in 1949 as placing a wrong emphasis on ' profit '.

Criticisms apart, there is in 'Rotary' today a volunteer organization for social service, a medium of friendly international contacts, a platform for hundreds of weekly addresses on topics of the day to men who may well be moulders of public opinion, a reservoir of candidates for the responsibilities of local government, and an almost incomparable means for the initiation of improving standards of business practice.

Rotarians fall short of their standards, but their faces are set towards the Good and the True. Does their Movement, then, carry with it any capacity for harm?

It could be said of it that its middle-class exclusiveness has certain undesirable effects in exacerbating class conflicts. At the annual conference of the Association at Blackpool in 1938, for example, the view was expressed (by a minority) that a higher fee for a tobacconist's excise licence would 'be welcomed by the trade and have an uplifting effect from a social point of view'. In spite of declared indifference as to class or creed, Rotary does not offer membership to the 'worker'. True, its 'classification list' provides for the admission to each Club of a representative of any 'Labour Organization' (i.e. trade union); but in view of the trade union official's relationship with his electors this can hardly be more than a gesture, and few men have found the dual rôle capable of fulfilment. 'I know that Rotary is used in business,' wrote a non-Rotarian workman in a letter to the Association in 1949, 'to help Rotarians to the detriment of their fellows : other things being equal, preference to Club members.' It would be strange indeed if there were not some truth in this quite typical complaint. But are these instances an adequate indication of any 'harm' that Rotary may incidentally do? It may be thought more probable that Rotary's harm lies in the possibility that social service without complete dedication, material as well as spiritual, may obscure the urgencies of inward goodness. 'The performance of public duty,' said Lord Russell in one of his 1949 *Reith Lectures*, 'is not the whole of what makes a good life. There is also the pursuit of private excellence. It is dangerous to allow social duty to dominate too completely our conception of what constitutes individual excellence.'

By this standard, true excellence is to be found only in the cloisters, the mission-stations, the leper colonies, and those fields of human service where men and women have forsworn all former

B

responsibilities and left them to others.   Is excellence denied to
those others ?   It was, on the contrary, their position as the
legatees of worldly responsibility that led Rotarians to seek
spiritual solace in what they have called ' Service '.   We shall see
that while in some instances they have failed lamentably, in others
they have succeeded admirably.

Chapter Two

THE FIRST BRITISH CLUBS

THE business men to whom the Rotary Movement was to appeal were, for the most part, members of the middle classes; men whose occupational interests would inform them of the trends and activities of 'big business' without offering the means of controlling events. They found in 1911, that, in spite of industrial production in other countries, British exports were increasing rapidly. Imports were rising, too, but more slowly than exports. The visible adverse trade balance was therefore smaller than at the beginning of the century; and the money value of exports to all countries—even to Germany—had in the same period roughly doubled. The competitive spirit in business was never greater.

A strong domestic reaction had set in, however, against Victorian beliefs and behaviour. England under the Queen had been a libertarian State, but its citizens had used their liberty to impose restraints of their own making; family disciplines, the authority of fathers, all-but-compulsory church-going, and the discouragement of all relaxations that did not loudly proclaim their educational or edifying value—these comprised a voluntary code of behaviour that fitted the social and economic system of industrialism. In the first decade of the new century there was a revolution that was almost sudden, the established beliefs were under continued attack from the disciples of Huxley, Arnold, Oscar Wilde, Ruskin, Bradlaugh, and other iconoclasts; the inevitable progress in which men had believed for fifty years appeared to have found better stimuli than the mere accumulation of wealth. The 'Rotary' idea arrived at a time when men of affairs were turning to Disraeli's view that 'there should be no property without duty', and away from the old Gradgrind philosophy that embraced a business system without friendship or loyalties. These features of the 'free' Edwardian period had, in their turn, produced a reaction in the shape of a 'popular' Press, which brought to bear on current ideas a facile verbal inventive-

ness and a cynical assessment of popular taste whose purpose was
to sell newspapers by the million without over-taxing the public
intelligence.   Alfred Harmsworth had started his *Daily Mail* in
1896, but it was in the nineteen-hundreds that its staccato narration
of ' human interest ' stories established its widespread readership
among the ' new illiterate ', and it was followed in many of its
antics by the *Daily Express*, the *Daily Mirror* and the *Daily Sketch*.
The arrival of ' Rotary ' as a new philosophy of altruism for
business men found no place in their columns.   It will be
important for our purposes to remember that in 1911, when broadcasting was a miracle of the unknown future, the mass of people
in this country were dependent for their knowledge of current
affairs (if they wanted it) on London-based newspapers of this
kind, and that the sober and honest provincial papers, where they
survived, were read only by the few.[1]

Liberalism, which had swept the polls in 1906, was still firmly
in office in 1911, supported to a large extent by political labour
and the trades unions : it had faithfully redeemed its election
promise to reverse the ' Taff Vale decision ' by which the House of
Lords had, in 1900, virtually outlawed trades unionism altogether;
but workmen in many trades were already showing the distrust
for trades union leaders that is so marked a feature of industrial
affairs today.   ' Unofficial ' strikes were frequent.   Tom Mann
and other left-wingers were preaching the gospel of ' direct
action ' : nothing real would ever be done for the workers ' until
they took their courage in both hands and did things for themselves '.   Accordingly a great dock strike was in progress in
London and the principal ports, rioting colliers on strike in South
Wales had been fired on by regular troops, taxi-drivers were
striking in London for the right to retain their ' extras ' when
they paid in a day's takings to their employers—and schoolboys
in London and the large towns were emulating their militant
parents by striking for an extra week's holiday, no homework, and
the abolition of caning !

*   *   *   *   *

Joseph Chamberlain's enthusiastic supporters were slowly
converting the country to Tariff Reform as a remedy for the

[1] Even in 1935 ' Rotary ' lamented, in its carefully compiled ' Rotary Viewpoint
in International Service ', the ' widespread ignorance of international politics and the
consequent failure to appreciate the effect on the problems of peace and war caused
by the ordinary happenings of day to day in our national business and political life '.

'dumping' here of foreign manufactures, but his policies competed for public attention with the problem of Home Rule for Ireland and the great constitutional crisis of the Parliament Act. *The Times* itself, anticipating Lloyd George's momentous reform of the House of Lords, suggested on 13th January, 1911, that their Lordships should themselves take steps involving the creation of 500 new peers. Mr. Balfour, in words that any Conservative speaker might use about 'nationalization' issues today, denied in the House of Commons that 'the electorate had given a mandate either for the Parliament Bill specifically or for the other measures suggested by the Government. Powers seized from the people,' he said, 'are being unconstitutionally used to carry out revolutions which the people have never sanctioned.'

The 'other measures' included Irish Home Rule and Tariff Reform. But 'whatever germs of future transformation of the social system these Bills might prove to contain, they were overshadowed entirely by the colossal scheme of National Insurance embodied in the Bill brought in by the Chancellor of the Exchequer on May 4th.' (And Income Tax at 1s. 2d. in the pound was already causing widespread and bitter complaint.) Business men were impressed by the Cadbury and Rowntree experiments in industrial relations, though the cynicism of the time found expression in Press correspondence suggesting that Quaker employers were making belated amends for the fact that their cocoa was for so long the product of slave labour in the plantations. There was an unmistakable trend towards the 'humanizing' of working conditions, which the Rotarian ideal was to foster and expand. But 'thirty per cent of existing pauperism', said Lloyd George when he introduced his State insurance scheme, 'is due to sickness, and a considerable further percentage to unemployment; and there is also a vast mass of unacknowledged destitution.' Barefooted children were still a common sight in the industrial towns. The women of the country, or that growing number of them who were politically minded, felt that men alone would never redress the social wrongs, and particularly the sex inequalities, that industrialism had produced, and militant Suffragism under the Pankhursts was carrying into effect a plan of propagandist violence and destruction.

* * * * *

Rotary Clubs had been spreading in the United States for six years, under the inspiration of Paul Harris, whose initiative had led to the establishment of the first of the Clubs in Chicago in 1905. Harris was dismayed to find that his 'fellowship' club of business men, whose main justification, as he saw it, was that it should do something for the community from which it drew its members, had become a self-help organization : it had a 'transactions register' containing the records of business deals effected by its members as a result of the weekly meetings; and the majority of the members saw it as a unique kind of 'closed shop' in which each man, free from the embarrassing presence of any-one of his own trade or profession, could exploit business 'contacts' in a comfortable glow of post-prandial goodwill. Unable to interest his fellow-members in the idea that service to the community should be the Club's main purpose (he had once considered naming it the 'Chicago Civic Club'), Harris turned his attention to the establishment of better Rotary Clubs in other American towns—San Francisco, Oakland, Seattle, Los Angeles, New York. The Chicago Club's opposition to this was strenuous. 'Rotary began here,' said the Chicago men, 'and it must remain a Chicago monopoly.' Some years elapsed before Harris found, in Chesley R. Perry (who joined the Club in 1908), a man of strength and purpose who would support his plans for 'extension'. The growth of the Movement thereafter was rapid. By 1910 there were sixteen Clubs, and they associated themselves in the National Association of Rotary Clubs of America, with Harris as President and Perry as Secretary. Chesley R. Perry retired from the position of 'Rotary International's' secretary in 1942; and Paul Harris, having watched his idea grow in forty years into a world movement with 6,800 Clubs and 327,000 members in eighty countries, died in 1947, a simple and well-beloved man dwarfed and somewhat bewildered by the magnitude of the thing into which his originally parochial conception had grown.

Anglo-American relations in 1911 were cordial, correct—and mutually baffling. Much has been written and published on both sides of the Atlantic, since America entered the Second World War in 1941, to guide the citizens of both countries towards a basis of mutual understanding. It need not be repeated here : together with personal contacts arising out of the war and a

growing awareness of economic identity, it has produced an
Anglo-American *entente* that did not exist in 1911. At that time,
it is safe to say, there was among ordinary people in this country
a conservative and even puritanical resistance to American ideas,
and it was the Americans' own presentation of them that
nourished the resistance : Hollywood had begun its export
programme. On the other hand, British business men with
trans-Atlantic contacts were receptive, interested, and in some
respects eager to copy; and it was to business men that the idea
of the Rotary Club was introduced.

*　　*　　*　　*　　*

No part of the world could have offered more fertile soil.
Englishmen had, at least since the sixteenth century, loved the
club as a centre of ease and conversation; the Bread Street Club
founded by Sir Walter Raleigh (and later known simply as the
Mermaid Tavern) was perhaps the first to emulate the clubs of
Ancient Rome which, having no committees or secretaries and no
club-houses of their own, had met at public baths and courtyards
by tacit appointment. It was Ben Jonson who drew up the rules
of the Apollo Club, which met at the Devil Tavern near Temple
Bar, and who dominated its meetings as Cicero ('the first club
bore') had dominated his Roman club sixteen hundred years
before and as Dryden was to do at Will's Club a century
after Jonson. Joseph Addison, writing in *The Spectator* on
10th March, 1710, remarked that

we take all occasions and pretences of forming ourselves into those
little nocturnal assemblies which are commonly known by the name of
clubs. When a set of men find themselves agree in any particular,
though never so trivial, they establish themselves into a kind of
fraternity and meet once or twice a week upon the account of such a
fantastic resemblance. I know a considerable market town in which
there was a club of fat men, that did not come together (as you may
well suppose) to entertain one another with sprightliness and wit, but
to keep one another in countenance. . . . This club, though it consisted but of fifteen persons, weighed above three ton.

In London, said Addison, there were even numerous 'street-
clubs' in which 'the chief inhabitants of the street conversed
together every night'. (He did not mention that these were also
places where the Londoner might seek refuge from the disorderly

attentions of other clubs like the notorious Mohocks, the Scourers, the Nickers, *et hoc omne genus*.) But

our modern celebrated clubs are founded upon eating and drinking, which are points wherein most men agree, and in which the learned and the illiterate, the dull and the airy, the philosopher and the buffoon, can all of them bear a part. When men are thus knit together by a love of society [he added more charitably] and not by a spirit of faction, and do not meet to censure or annoy those that are absent but to enjoy one another, when they are thus combined for their own improvement or for the good of others, or at least to relax themselves from the business of the day by an innocent and cheerful conversation, there may be something very useful in these little institutions and establishments.

There may indeed; and Rotarians, in due course, were to see their possibilities. But Addison concluded his essay with an account of a club that foreshadowed ' Rotary ' itself, with certain prescribed eccentricities to take the place of the leg-pulling ' heartiness ' which, in 1911, was to give American Rotary Clubs some unpropitious advance publicity.

I cannot forbear concluding this paper [he wrote] with a scheme of laws I met with upon a wall in a little ale-house. How I came thither I may inform my reader at a more convenient time. These laws were enacted by a knot of artisans and mechanics who used to meet every night : and as there is something in them which gives us a pretty picture of low life, I shall transcribe them word for word :

Rules to be Observed in the Twopenny Club, erected in this Place for the Preservation of Friendship and Good Neighbourhood

1. Every member at his first coming in shall lay down his twopence.
2. Every member shall fill his pipe out of his own box.
3. If any member absents himself, he shall forfeit a penny for the use of the club, unless in case of sickness or imprisonment.
4. If any member swears or curses, his neighbour may give him a kick upon the shins.
5. If any member tells stories in the club that are not true, he shall forfeit for every third lie a halfpenny.
6. If any member strikes another wrongfully, he shall pay his club for him.
7. If any member brings his wife into the club, he shall pay for whatever she drinks or smokes.
8. If any member's wife comes to fetch him home from the club, she shall speak to him without the door.

9. If any member calls another a cuckold, he shall be turned out of the club.
10. *None shall be admitted to the club that is of the same trade with any member of it.*
11. None of the club shall have his clothes or shoes made or mended, but by a brother member.
12. No non-juror [i.e. no person who refused in 1689 to take the oath of allegiance to William and Mary] shall be capable of being a member.

The exclusiveness of this odd assembly, its status as a ' classification ' club by definition in Rule No. 10, the mutual assistance motive suggested by Rule No. 11, and the discrimination against current undesirables so bluntly stated in Rule No. 12—these features suggest that the Rotary Club idea was far from new to this country in 1911, and that its favourable reception was historically assured.

*   *   *   *   *

But it was to Irishmen that it first appealed on this side of the Atlantic. Paul Harris, who had just succeeded in establishing a Rotary Club in Winnipeg (the first outside the United States), was discussing the formation of a London Club with Mr. Harvey Wheeler of Boston, Massachusetts, who had a towel-supply business in London. With two other enthusiasts they were proceeding with the London project and contemplating another in Manchester, when to their astonishment they learned, in August, 1911, that a Rotary Club already existed in Dublin.

Mr. Stuart Morrow, a former Rotarian of San Francisco, had convened and presided over a meeting of Dublin business men which, on 22nd February, 1911, formally set up the Rotary Club of Dublin. He then took the idea to Belfast and, with great pertinacity, gathered from its trades and professions a nucleus of men to form, on 24th July, 1911, the Rotary Club of Belfast. Harris thought he saw in Stuart Morrow a zealot after his own heart. He encouraged Morrow, by correspondence, to continue the missionary work, and Clubs were duly formed (by the efforts of Morrow and others) in Manchester, Glasgow, Edinburgh, Birmingham, and Liverpool.

But a Rotary Club acquires true membership of the ' International ' only when it has received its Charter from the Chicago headquarters of the Movement; and, in applying for charters, the new Clubs, probably through administrative or secretarial delays, lost their original order of chronological precedence. The 'charter numbers' of these first Clubs give them, in this sense, a fallacious order of seniority to which Irish Rotarians will call your attention as they would to an attack on their claim to the nativity of St. Patrick (who was born in Scotland). The London Club is listed in the *Directory of Rotary Clubs in Great Britain and Ireland* as No. 50, the lowest number outside the North American Continent. Glasgow is No. 60, Edinburgh 62, Dublin 65, Manchester 66, Belfast 67, Liverpool 80, and Birmingham 108. The Irish contempt for statistics has seldom found sterner nourishment; but it is at least admitted that Dublin postponed affiliation (probably because the amount of the fee had not been decided) until 4th April, 1913, and was 'chartered' on 2nd June, 1913—more than two years after its formation. Belfast was not chartered until 4th May, 1914.

It has since been alleged that Morrow's missionary zeal had a material core, that he was selling memberships in the new Clubs for a guinea apiece, and (according to a report compiled in 1934 by the Social Science Committee of the University of Chicago) [1] this was the way in which he was making his living. The Liverpool Club records that Morrow, as organizing secretary for the time being, had a salary of one guinea a week and was paid a 'bonus' of half the two-guinea entrance fee of every new member he obtained. Plans to send him to Australia and New Zealand as a one-man 'extension committee' with the world as his territory were, whatever the reason, incontinently dropped, and 'extension' began to assume the more decorous and satisfactory form described in Chapter Three.

*   *   *   *   *

But meanwhile American Rotarians, confronted with the evidence of Harris's success and determination in spreading the Movement beyond American soil, had to recognize that it was no longer nationalistic. The National Association of Rotary Clubs of America was now a misnomer; and in 1912, with the change of

[1] 'Rotary? A University Group Looks at the Rotary Club of Chicago'. University of Chicago Press, 1934. The payments to Morrow are also recorded in the minutes of some of the earlier clubs.

title to 'The International Association of Rotary Clubs', there began a careful policy, steadfastly maintained ever since, of preserving the international character of the Movement by every device of precept and administration that could suggest itself to the constitution-loving American mind. It was to meet with parochial difficulties; and there were occasions, as will be related in Chapter Five, when it led to sharp exchanges of view between the parental headquarters in Chicago and countries jealous of their national forms of sociological expression. But the feeling in the minds of men throughout the world was already impatient, on the whole, of nationalistic emphasis, and the future of Rotary International, as a convenient expression of world-fellowship, was assured. The world had not yet been drawn into the two vast war-camps of 1914. Men were yet to learn how the desperate friendships of war could be endangered in the quarrels of a 'victorious' peace.

Before the war began, the eight 'founder' Clubs had formed themselves into the British Association of Rotary Clubs, a step which, although it had been regarded uneasily from Chicago, was officially ratified at an International Convention at Houston in June, 1914. The B.A.R.C. was an autonomous administration. Its original constitution did not impose on the eight Clubs any affiliation to the 'International', though affiliation was recommended. Chicago made an important gesture, which at the same time gave discreet emphasis to the international aspect, by appointing a British Rotarian as a vice-president of the International Association. At that time there were some Clubs in Great Britain that were affiliated members of the International and some that were not; but in 1916 the British Clubs adopted a new constitution requiring that all should be affiliated to both organizations. The compromise was to last through the war years and result in a more logical dovetailing in 1921, acceptable alike to the American taste for centralization and to the British insistence on quasi-autonomy.

Chapter Three

THE CRUSADE

By 1915 the urge to get more and more towns to form Rotary Clubs had assumed the character of a crusade; and it was pursued with an enthusiasm which, in time, was seen to be lacking in discrimination. For a year or two the Movement grew almost spontaneously, as it were by self-propagation. It is said by Rotarians old enough to remember that towns without Rotary Clubs began to demand them; though it should be borne in mind that ' towns ', in this sense, means local communities of men in the executive, managerial class, markedly similar in their attitude towards public problems, as exclusive of the real captains of industry as of members of the working class or of left-wing politicians, of bohemian intellectuals, of declared atheists, of scholars, and of the independent well-to-do.

The demand made club-formation a comparatively simple matter. The extension methods that had been attributed, rightly or wrongly, to Stuart Morrow were at this time being used in the United States to propagate a somewhat similar association known as the Lions Club Movement—salaried ' field representatives ' of ' Lions International ' were setting up new clubs by high-pressure methods that were producing a remarkable percentage of failures. By contrast, Rotary International stated in 1933 that ' less than two per cent of all the Rotary Clubs ever established have gone out of existence ', and the reasons it gave for those failures were (a) that the Clubs concerned had been formed in ' boom towns ' of the kind that have risen and fallen in American territorial development, (b) that they succumbed to the ' depression ' of the nineteen-thirties, and (c) that they were killed by mere boredom. In this country there have been less than half a dozen failures. But there were early instances in which Clubs were formed at the instigation of misguided enthusiasts who thought it sufficient to call together the leading personalities of a township and call the result a Rotary Club. In some cases it was found that a Rotary

Club had restricted its membership to Freemasons (a practice specifically condemned at the time of the Rotary Convention at Edinburgh in 1921). When news of such a formation reached the British Association of Rotary Clubs, representatives of that body would bear down upon these unwitting traducers of the name of ' Rotary ' and inform them that they were not a Rotary Club in any acceptable sense of the word, and that they must either begin *de novo* with their Club formation or abstain from using the name. It is a curious fact that Rotarians in Britain have repeatedly considered and rejected proposals to incorporate their association as a legal entity; and although they employ patent agents to keep them informed of any cases where the name ' Rotary ' (or the Rotary emblem) is used without authority, and are prepared to take up any such challenge to their exclusive use, neither the name nor the emblem is specifically protected. But it is probable that any association of men using the name without authority both could and would be restrained by the issue, at the suit of ' R.I.B.I.', of a High Court injunction restraining them from its further use.

The newly-formed British Association of Rotary Clubs appointed a Board of Directors (two delegates from each Club) which made a practice of holding its meetings in different cities. The alarming course which the war was taking from 1914 to 1916 had called into being that inchoate patriotic doggedness that has so often distinguished the British people in adversity, and there was scope for the formation of Rotary Clubs as nuclei of national service in many forms. A small ' extension committee ' of the B.A.R.C. inspired the formation of Clubs in Newcastle upon Tyne, Leeds, Leicester, Aberdeen, Portsmouth, Perth, Bristol, Cardiff, Llanelly, Nottingham, Derby, Southampton, and some smaller towns. All these duly affiliated themselves to the B.A.R.C. The Movement continued to spread in this way, and even more in response to enquiries from townships throughout Great Britain.

In 1918 it was found necessary to regionalize the responsibility for new formations. Great Britain and Ireland were therefore divided into six Districts, and selected Clubs in each District were given the responsibility of ' extension work ' in that District. There then grew up, in response to the need for an authoritatively-prescribed *modus operandi*, the system of ' extension ' which is operated today. A brief examination of that system follows : it merits the historian's attention as the fruit of early experience

and the means by which ill-organized and 'unrotarian' Club
formations are now avoided.

*   *   *   *   *

Each of the Districts, of which there are now eighteen, was
listed as a District of Rotary International (*not* of 'R.I.B.I.'),
and appointed a District Extension Committee.[1] The Committee's
function was to study the District territory and come to decisions
as to the towns which seemed likely to offer the earliest opportunities for forming new Clubs; and thereafter to 'survey' each
town in accordance with the terms of a detailed questionnaire.
What kind of place was the surveyed town 'vocationally'?
What were its proposed territorial limits, and were they most
suitable both for the proposed Club and with an eye to neighbouring Clubs of the future? Were there enough 'classifications' in
the town?—a question that might rule out a purely dormitory
place in which the only businesses were those of the few indispensable shops and the only professions those of the doctor,
the parson, and the schoolmaster. If the 'founder members'
left the Club after a year or two, would there be sufficient
'classifications' to replace them? Were there several possible
meeting-places for the Club, so that the weekly lunch-meeting
which was to be its essential feature would not be at the mercy or
caprice of a single café-proprietor or innkeeper?

Rotarians believed it to be of the utmost importance that while
this 'survey' was going on no one outside the Movement should
be allowed to learn that the formation of a Rotary Club was
contemplated. In particular, no one must at this stage be
approached and 'sounded' as to his willingness to become a
founder-member. They were doubtless well-advised in this, since
the rejection of a candidate for membership might, when it almost
inevitably became known among leading townsmen, expose him
to that 'ridicule and contempt' upon which libel actions can be
founded. The result of the survey was reported to the Extension
Committee of the national association ('R.I.B.I.'), which, working
from a wider experience, approved or disapproved the proposed
formation. Approval was indispensable, and was regarded as
the firmest possible foundation. It was not lightly given, and it
represented the conclusions of the association's 'elder states-

[1] But see footnote, p. 29.

men '.   It authorized the formation of a Club of not less than
fifteen and not more than thirty-five founder-members (a minimum of twenty was preferred); the maximum was prescribed in
order that ' all members may get on terms of fellowship with
each other before still more are added '.   Every available scrap of
information about the professional and business men of the town
was then considered, and the local Committee selected the one
whose influence and co-operation they most desired as founder-
member number one.   He was interviewed by two of the
committee-men; the purposes of a Rotary Club were explained
to him, the responsibilities of individual members being specially
emphasized; and he received the gratifying information that he
was being approached because he was THE man of his business or
profession in the town upon whom the choice of Rotary had
fallen.   Few men were found to withstand this : and their enhanced self-respect was further nourished when, having agreed
to the project, they were asked to name two or three other men
in the town who might make good Rotarians or to pronounce
upon the qualities of two or three whom the Committee already
had in mind.

The approach to number two was identical, except that he could
not be mollified with the statement that he was the first one
approached, and he must be told that number one had already
been recruited.   But now that there were two members, their
agreement as to the suitability of number three must be obtained
and recorded before number three was duly interviewed.   And so
the process continued.   The first three or four founder members
were called together at a meeting, and with the *Outline of Classifications* before them they discussed suitable townsmen to be
canvassed.

The *Outline of Classifications* is a remarkable compilation : it
justifies a digression.   It alphabetically lists seventy-seven ' major
classifications ' from Aeronautic Equipment to Wool, and sub-
divides each into ' minor classifications ' appropriate to the
various branches or processes.   Compiled in Chicago with a view
to its use in other languages, its terminology has nevertheless
a strongly American flavour, which draws added piquance from
such juxtapositions as ' Beverages, Broadcasting, Building,
Burial ', or ' Real Estate, Recreation, Refrigeration, Religion '.
The ' minor classifications ' under ' Religion ' illustrate admirably,

however, the liberality of this world-wide association. They are listed, again with the rigid impartiality of the alphabet, as Buddhism, Christianity (Established Church,[1] Free Churches,[1] and Roman Catholicism), Confucianism, Hinduism, Judaism, Mohammedanism, Taoism, and Zoroastrianism. This universality should be borne in mind later, when the failure of ' Rotary ' to champion sectarian causes is under discussion.

Very early in this process of assembling founder-members, the weekly lunch meeting began.

After all [urged the Provisional Formation Committee], if this Club is formed, you gentlemen will be meeting regularly every week at lunch. Why not start now ? We can then agree upon a few names every week. As we succeed, the size of our luncheon meeting will grow until we have all the prospective founder members we require. Meanwhile, those who are uncertain about their ability to attend a weekly Club lunch can try it out before they are finally committed to membership. Also, we get to know each other better and gradually absorb the new ones as they come along. Then, too, we can try out a few meeting places in advance.[2]

The main principles of Club formation are summarised thus for the guidance of Provisional Formation Committees :

1. Prospective members should be active business men whose places of business are located within the territorial limits of the proposed new Club.
2. Retired business men are not eligible unless they qualify as Past Service Members or Senior Active Members.
3. Keep the average age of members as low as possible, by bringing in younger men.[3]
4. Prospective members should be earnestly requested not to mention Rotary membership to any of their friends, unless their friends' names have been approved and agreed by the members already elected.
5. Avoid cliques and do not necessarily select men who are in the public eye. See that the same members do not sit together each week.
6. The classification of the firm by whom a person is employed fixes the qualification, not the duties which that particular person per-

---

[1] In the main American ' Outline ' these are respectively ' Orthodox Catholicism ' and ' Protestantism '. The British edition has made a few concessions to insular trade description, though ' Real Estate ', for example, remains, to the occasional embarrassment of surveyors who belong to Rotary Clubs and have read ' Babbitt '.

[2] *How to Form a Rotary Club*, pp. 24, 25. R.I.B.I., 1948.

[3] The average age is, in fact, probably fifty.

forms for the company; e.g., an accountant as a full-time member of the staff of a shoe manufacturing company takes that company's classification, not ' Accountancy '.

7. Classifications mainly divide themselves into three groups : industrial, distributive, and professional. Care should be taken to have a well-balanced membership, and in selecting classifications each week cognizance should be taken of the existing division under these main Groups.

    *   *   *   *   *

In the nineteen-thirties, extension committees began to encounter opposition. ' Our town is too small,' they were sometimes told. They replied that any community containing enough men of good character in sufficient trades and professions to provide twenty men was a suitable place for a Rotary Club. ' But our town is different.' Of course, said the Rotarians : all towns are different. In over 6,000 towns Rotary has proved its adaptability to these community differences. ' Well, the time isn't opportune.' But excellent Clubs had been organized in many places in face of this objection—the more difficult the local situation the greater the necessity of a Rotary Club to the community. ' Our town doesn't need a Rotary Club.' No one outside the Movement, replied the Rotarians, was able to make this statement : he did not know what Rotary was. ' We shan't get anything out of Rotary.' Not materially, was the reply : Rotary did not provide opportunities for material gain. It existed to give men of public spirit the chance to serve the Community. ' But a Rotary Club would clash with other existing organizations.' Experience had proved, on the contrary, that in a great number of cases Rotary had strengthened and stimulated existing service organizations, and had often co-operated with such bodies. It never clashed with existing service movements. ' But if you select one man to represent his classification, you will create ill-will.' The fallacy of this contention was said to be proved by the fact that thousands of Rotary Clubs had existed harmoniously in hundreds of communities for many years. In many cases the Clubs, because of their classification basis, had been able to reconcile hostile factions in a town : a Rotarian was expected to serve as a liaison officer between the Club and the men in his vocation. ' Well, it is impossible to keep the attendance rule—a minimum of 60 per cent lunch-meetings every

c

year.' The busiest man, said the Rotarians in disposing of this, was in practice the best attender.

But the reasons why men join Rotary Clubs have changed; as a generality they have, indeed, changed more than once. In 1911, some men would join because they were what the Americans have called ' natural-born joiners ' : some men will join anything. Some were attracted by the pleasant associations, others by a sense of acquired prestige, and yet others by the belief, amounting in some cases to certainty, that membership of the local Rotary Club would be a business asset. Comparatively few who joined for the last-named reason remained Rotarians for that reason. They were disillusioned when they found that any attempt to turn a Rotary Club into a co-operative trading association would have ill-effects upon their future trade with non-Rotarians. But it is highly desirable for a bank manager to know the personalities in his local business community : a bank manager may be a friendly man, but he should also be a discreetly inquisitive man. It is necessary to the branch manager of an insurance company that he should be similarly well-informed about people. In a score of comparable occupations, contact with the business and profes-sional world is never complete; no opportunity should be lost of extending it. Rotary Clubs offered this contact, and Rotary Clubs were joined by a considerable proportion of their members for business reasons; but if ' business ' is to be understood as meaning a healthier profit-and-loss account, it is important to recognize that any financial advantage of Rotary membership goes to the man whose occupation touches a small number of clients or customers paying large fees or commissions (lawyers, estate agents, etc.), rather than the tradesman who depends on a large clientèle paying individually small sums. Today there are un-doubtedly men who join a Rotary Club because it affords them opportunities for social service in an atmosphere that is not noticeably ' pious '. And there are men who remain in the Clubs because membership facilitates self-expression, and gives them poise and confidence in public appearance through speaking and presiding at the meetings.

*   *   *   *   *

Fellowship, in fact, though it was the original call, was not enough. Rotary Clubs had become important centres of social endeavour. But their activities were as yet ill co-ordinated, and co-ordination must be the concern of the Association, of the central authority to which all the Clubs were affiliated. In the mid-nineteen twenties there began, accordingly, a campaign of ' education ' in the ' aims and objects ' of the Movement, beginning with the re-drafting of the purposes of ' Rotary ' in the form set out on page 5, and continuing with the issue from headquarters of carefully-drafted pamphlets designed to impose a pattern of behaviour on the Clubs. The primary emphasis at this time was on ' vocational service '; the builder, the dentist, the baker could best serve the community by being a good builder, dentist, or baker, charging ' fair ' prices and shunning ' unethical ' practices. Sydney Pascall, a manufacturing confectioner and one of the Movement's strongest and most respected leaders, was an enthusiastic advocate of ethical ' codes ' for the various businesses and professions, such as had been compiled in prolific detail by Rotary International on the basis of American experience. An urgent and eloquent conference speaker, he carried the Movement with him in a mood of legislative enthusiasm which, however, was not to last. Rotarians in Britain had Common Law minds. They inherited, that is to say, the well-known British antipathy to rules and regulations which, throughout Parliamentary history, had left the settlement of disputes and the prescription of conduct to His Majesty's Judges, who were supposed to draw upon hereditary funds of wisdom bequeathed to them by the light of Nature. Pascall's ' codes ' remain in the *Proceedings* of the Annual Conferences among the records of their acclamation, but they have not been officially adopted. Instead, the ethical behaviour of the individual Rotarian in his business or profession is suggested in a pamphlet on ' Vocational Service ' published by ' R.I.B.I.' and revised from time to time. This lays down broad principles concerning the Rotarian's relationship with his employers, with his competitors, with those from whom he buys, and with his customers or clients. It urges co-operation with and fair dealing for employees (paying special regard to the bewilderments of the young), profit-sharing schemes, production committees, training in industry, and exemplary standards in wages and conditions of employment. It enjoins co-operation with competitors in design and market research, with the Government in providing full employment, and with Chambers of Commerce and Trade. It eschews bribery, business with firms of ill-repute, and cut-price competition, and commends the honouring of contracts and the prompt settlement of accounts. It extols efficiency, truth in advertising, and the æsthetic importance of good premises, manufactures, and printing, and condemns any tendency in Rotarians to seek or expect special business favours from each other.

Every Club was to have a Vocational Service Committee, charged with the duty of propagating these ideals and devising means for their fulfilment. But it must also have a Club Service Committee to deal in a more or less uniform manner with the management of the Club and its purposes of fellowship and recreation, a Community Service Committee to guide and further its welfare and cultural work outside the Club, and (though this came later, under the influence of the work being done by the League of Nations) an International Service Committee for the furtherance of international amity.

These four Committees absorbed, in each Club, the work of a host of smaller committees which had been working without national co-ordination or mutual resemblance. The new Committees provided an accessible target for exhortation from the headquarters of a movement which was now becoming fully organized on a national basis, within the framework of the 'International'. The International itself, in 1927, adopted the new British scheme of 'aims and objects committees' which is probably the greatest contribution this country, or indeed any country, has made to Rotary. 'R.I.B.I.'s' national publications may be said to have become effective from that time. In 1915 it had begun the publication of *The Rotary Wheel*, a monthly magazine devoted to the interests and purposes of 'Rotary' in Great Britain and Ireland (it has since changed its name to *Rotary Service*). Its first issue set the pattern for the self-criticism which was to follow by publishing a contributed article on the following theme : 'We Rotarians are either limited in our membership so as to obtain the benefits of business exchange, or else there is no reason whatever for the limitations.' It also reported a resolution of the British Association of Rotary Clubs that proclaimed a policy of intensive propaganda :

Clubs are recommended to give all possible publicity to the Rotary Movement, by means of newspaper reports of meetings and by schemes of public, civic, and patriotic work, and other means whereby the Movement may be brought to the notice of outsiders. Only in this way can Rotary spread through the Country and new Clubs be formed.[1]

This statement proved to be of doubtful validity. Press publicity was to have little measurable effect on the growth of the Movement. The earliest mention of ' Rotary ' in *The Times* was a report on 13th June, 1918, of an entertainment given to wounded soldiers by the Rotary Club of London; and by that time, as we have seen, a campaign for the founding of new Clubs was taking shape through the efforts of the District Councils, whose work consisted almost entirely of ' extension '. It has since been the concern of District Extension Committees.[2]

The Rotary Movement first reached the ' popular ' Press in 1921, when the holding of Rotary International's first European convention took place in Edinburgh; and the popular Press, whose readers would scarcely notice a sober reference to Rotary idealism as they hurried through to the cricket news and the racing results, were halted by the discovery that Rotary had provided the Press with a ' feature story ' which it could fall upon with glee. This portrayed the group behaviour of the American delegates in the streets of Edinburgh. Those who know the gregarious American business man and have seen the lighter side of his ' Assemblies ' and ' Conventions ' will perhaps realize what was then purveyed to a British newspaper public which was at first incredulous, then outraged, and then contemptuous. The Rotarian was seen to be coeval with the pole-squatter, the comic-strip buffoon, and the man who propelled a pea-nut from New York to Detroit with the tip of his nose.

These external manifestations of the boy-like spirit of America [wrote the then General Secretary of R.I.B.I. in later years] afforded the London Press its principal material so far as the Rotary Convention was concerned, despite the fact that the actual speeches and discussions in the Convention Hall afforded excellent copy, suggesting as they did the possibilities of a movement of men of goodwill as a means to cement the Peace, and supplement the work of the newly-founded

[1] *The Rotary Wheel*, January, 1915, p. 21.
[2] Though, at the time of writing, the work in each District has been experimentally entrusted to a single ' District Extension Officer ', who works in constant touch with the District Chairman. Extension was proceeding too rapidly for healthy development.

League of Nations. . . . It would now be a labour of years to persuade the British Press that Rotary really meant anything serious.[1]

Side by side with *The Rotary Wheel* was the 'International's' own journal, *The Rotarian*, published from Chicago and circulated throughout the world. The various Rotary 'Districts' in Great Britain and Ireland produced their own journals giving fuller details of local achievements and objectives. Ireland led with a magazine modestly calling itself *Cogs*, by identification of the Club as a unit with the cogs on the symbolic 'Rotary Wheel'; first published as the Dublin Club's own journal on 17th November, 1913, and later adopted as the journal of the entire Irish 'District', it is two years older than the *Rotary Wheel* itself. London followed in 1916 with *The London Rotarian*, a forty-page journal devoting half its space (as was common with Rotary literature at the time but is now sternly discountenanced) to advertisements of Rotarians' businesses and professions. An excellent quarterly magazine that failed to survive the Second World War was called *Service* (or, more fully, *Service in Life and Work*). Published by the Association of Great Britain and Ireland, this was not a declared 'Rotary platform', but a first-class quarterly review offering articles by distinguished publicists on topics of the day, and contenting itself (as does, for example, the *Christian Science Monitor*) with journalism of high integrity and the utmost catholicity of interest as a means to the 'preparation of the soil'.

The public Press, as we have seen, paid little regard to Rotary affairs and aspirations until the close of the First World War. The first *Times* article to do so, indeed, appeared on 3rd June, 1921, when, under the headlines 'Fair Dealing and Service—Rotary Clubs' Ideals and Record', it reviewed the decisions arrived at by the Edinburgh Convention. From that time the Rotary Movement's increasing acceptance as a serious social phenomenon was reflected in all the more responsible journals. Viscount Burnham, continuing as owner of the *Daily Telegraph* his father's interest in philanthropy and social welfare, took an interest in the Rotary Movement, though not himself a Rotarian. He was persuaded, moreover, that by devoting some space to Rotary news he would attract readership among the growing

[1] Vivian Carter, *The Romance of Rotary in London*, p. 35.

number of business men who were Rotarians; and for several years from 1927 onwards a weekly column of Rotary news was contributed to the *Daily Telegraph* by Vivian Carter, then general secretary of the Association. The speeches delivered at Rotary lunches now provide regular copy for local newspapers, and important pronouncements by distinguished guest speakers at the larger Clubs are noticed in the National Press. Rotary lunches have, in fact, become known as convenient platforms for countless causes, and the secretaries of Club Service Committees, in engaging speakers, have learned to discriminate accordingly.

*   *   *   *   *

In the First World War the members of the Clubs were, for the most part, above military age. But the resolution passed in 1915 (see pages 28–9), with its call to 'schemes of patriotic work', reflects the feeling of corporate responsibility in the affairs of the nation that was to be expected from men of the kind to be found in Rotary Clubs. Some Clubs joined their local special constabulary *en masse*. Others organized 'flag-days' for war-relief purposes, entertained large assemblies of disabled troops, equipped Red Cross ambulances, provided and maintained hospital beds and acted as hospital orderlies, and 'adopted' war orphans. They raised and equipped many of the so-called 'Bantam Battalions' of men for service in the Territorial Army. (These were men of short stature who were excluded from the Territorial Regiments because, in the first wave of war enthusiasm, those still-autonomous organizations were imposing rigid standards of physique as an expression of pride in their long-delayed recognition. The 'Bantams' were men anxious to serve, disappointed at their rejection, waiting for someone to organize and equip them, and destined to give a good account of themselves as units before the monstrous casualty lists of Loos and the Somme relaxed the standards of recruitment.) The Rotary Clubs also set up 'information kiosks' in the streets of large cities for the guidance and help of visiting forces and refugees, and established numerous refugee hostels which they staffed and supervised throughout the war. A typical enterprise was the supervision by London Rotarians, every Tuesday night, of the famous 'Eagle Hut' erected by the U.S.A. military authorities in the Strand for American troops passing through London. Hundreds of

Rotarians, in all parts of the country, opened their homes to refugees from invaded Belgium and beleaguered France. And when the men came back from the war to Mr. Lloyd George's oft-derided ' land fit for heroes ', to the disillusion of a ' victor's peace ' in a world made one by international trade, it was Rotarian business men who, perhaps more than anyone, made openings for them in employment and in newly-capitalized businesses on their own. ' Jobs for Demobs ', as Rotarians were led by their love of slogans to call it, was a campaign in which ' Community Service ' and ' Vocational Service ' found urgent and practical expression.

The years that followed were to provide tests of ingenuity and optimism that few could then foresee. And in the meantime the Rotary Movement in this country, with only occasional and emergency contacts with the ' International ' and Chicago, had grown strong, self-reliant—and distinctively British.

Chapter Four

THE 'DISTRICTS'

THIS 'distinctively British' quality was destined to survive even the resumption of full contacts with Chicago and the American system of organization. The original 'British Association of Rotary Clubs' was governed by a Board of Directors, consisting of two members from each Club; and the eight 'founder clubs' thus elected a Board of only sixteen men. But by 1918 there were thirty Clubs and sixty Directors, and moreover the six 'Districts' into which the thirty Clubs had been grouped in that year were already seen to be unwieldy. The whole of Scotland was one District. Ireland was another—'partition' was unknown to Irish Rotarians. The whole of England north of the Humber was another, and a fourth was the entire south and south-west, including South Wales. At 'District' level the co-ordination of policy, and particularly the business of supervising 'extension', were necessarily on a more intimate scale than the remoter government from headquarters; and yet the size of the Districts and their own problems of travel and expenses made them, from the headquarter's viewpoint, awkward children. A further 'partition' and re-grouping must be resorted to if control from the centre was not to grow progressively weaker as the Clubs grew numerically stronger.

In 1922, after the International Convention at Los Angeles, the Secretary of the 'British Association of Rotary Clubs' (Vivian Carter) was invited to spend some time in the Chicago office and study the American organization. He found that each District Governor, despite the enormous distances involved, visited every Club in his District at least once during his year of elected office. District Conferences were 'statutory', and well-attended; and the decisions of Chicago upon matters of policy were observed throughout the Clubs. The secret was an annual 'Assembly', held immediately before each annual Convention, at which the District Governors took an intensive course of 'Rotary Instruc-

33

tion ': a serious-minded session, divorced from the fun-and-games atmosphere which sometimes characterized the Convention itself—though the latter had its value in getting the delegates together from all parts of a vast continent.   They then returned to their Districts and summoned District ' Assemblies ', at which the official policy for the ensuing year, reflecting to a large extent the trend of social and international affairs, was passed on to representatives of the Clubs.   At that time the British ' Aims and Objects Plan ' was not yet born, and in the absence of its prescribed continuity a fresh programme was drawn up every year.   Carter found, among the American delegates, that the men most concerned with the Rotary Movement as a serious organization for social service regarded the ' Assemblies ' as its life-blood, even if the Conferences were an indispensable social complement. Today the distinction is equally valid in this country.

The British Clubs decided in 1923 to re-define their District boundaries, increasing the number of Districts to sixteen, each with a Chairman and an elected Council. A District Council came to consist of two delegates from each Club in the District, a Chairman, vice-chairmen numbering not more than four, a secretary, a treasurer, and the three preceding chairmen.   From that point the District Councils, with a traditionally British appetite for self-government, seemed to be assuming a status hardly subordinate to that of the General Council of ' R.I.B.I.', the governing body of the Movement in this country.   By 1928 it was possible for the President (Dr. Thomas Stephenson) to say that

in some cases there is a tendency to carry this seriousness just a little too far—for the District Councils to regard themselves somewhat in the light of a Ratepayers' Association, whose sole function is to criticize the governing body.   In other words, there is a tendency in places for the tail to wag the dog.

Further

The District Council [says the official handbook that purports to describe and limit its functions] is an administrative body for District affairs, intermediate between the General Council and the clubs and working under the general supervision of the General Council.[1]

[1] *A Guide for District Executives*.   R.I.B.I., 1935, revised 1948.

And so it is. But the tendency for the tail to wag the dog has increased; and it was the practice of holding District Conferences, beginning in 1923 (District 'Assemblies' did not begin until some years later), that accentuated the process of devolution.

Most of the Districts hold their Conferences in the autumn, almost invariably at week-ends and within a period of five or six weeks. Groups of them are thus going on simultaneously, a fact which, by making it impossible for the President to attend them all, removes them still farther from the reach of the parental arm. He is represented at the Conferences by officers of the Association.

The District Conferences began as one-day meetings in some town conveniently situated for all attending; but later they lasted for three days, and might be attended by more than 500 Rotarians, many of whom brought their wives. Accordingly, these took place at holiday resorts and health spas, not, as critics of the Movement suggested, because the occasion was a mere 'jamboree' of feasting and 'fellowship' in picturesque surroundings, but because it was only in such places that hotel accommodation on such a scale was to be found : few members at a Conference saw more of the town or its attractions than the streets between railway station, hotel, and conference hall (though there were always a number who treated the occasion as a week-end of jollification); and for the three days, immured in conference rooms during weather that was frequently a tempting summons to open-air pursuits, they devoted themselves to crowded programmes of speeches, discussions, and plans for the coming year, allotting perhaps two evenings to an entertainment and dance with their wives and daughters.

*　　　*　　　*　　　*　　　*

It was the purpose of the District 'Assembly', as distinct from the District Conference, to pass on to the newly-elected committee-men of the Clubs the National Association's plans for the year, the means by which those plans were to be carried into effect, and the chapter-and-verse basis that related them to the 'aims and objects' of Rotary. It was an annual academy where the teachers, themselves freshly instructed at a national 'Assembly' of a similar kind, taught lesser teachers. The national Assembly had heard addresses from the President and from the Chairmen of the various main Committees—Club, Vocational, Community, and International Service, Extension, Finance, and so on. It dispersed to repeat those addresses, at District Assemblies, to the Club men who were to do the spade work. One result of this system was that to hold 'District' office in any capacity for a year or two was to hear those addresses given, with little textual variation though with greatly differing eloquence, over and over again. Little sign appeared that this was found wearisome; and the impartial observer, who might have wondered what each man in those packed audiences was thinking as the familiar doctrines were declaimed, would have been told by the majority that the ritual was necessary 'for the new men' and did no harm to the old: the good Rotarian could take it. A minority would say that the speakers were enjoying the fruits of office, the right to a platform and an audience: Rotarians were determined speech-makers. And the same sophisticated minority would explain that the audience then proceeded to enjoy the smaller fruits of lesser office by handing it all on at District Assemblies—where-after the Club committee-men should, in turn, hand it on to their constituents at 'Club Assemblies'. 'Use not vain repetitions, as the heathen do,' said St. Matthew; 'for they think they shall be heard for their much speaking.' But St. Matthew was not a Rotarian; and these repetitions, as the following chapters will show, were by no means in vain. Why, it may be asked, could all this exhortation not be conveyed by printed pamphlet or circular? The answer involves the analogy of the horse taken to the water: it was, but you could not be satisfied that the pamphlets were read. And where they failed, the 'inspirational' speeches and the almost devotional atmosphere of their reception could, and did, to a large extent succeed.

*   *   *   *   *

It was at 'District level' that the financial structure of the Movement could best be seen in operation. A District had two sources of revenue—a 'Block Grant' from the funds of the Movement, and (though this was not universally used) money raised by a voluntary *per capita* contribution from members of Clubs in the District. The latter was strictly voluntary (the District Councils had no authority to impose levies), and any Club was free to refuse contributions to District funds. The

'Block Grant' covered (besides stationery and sundries) the expenses of the chairman, vice-chairmen, secretary, and treasurer. It included the hire of accommodation for Assemblies, District Councils, and District Committees, but *not* for District Conferences, the cost of which was defrayed by those attending them in person. The expenses of the chairman and his vice-chairmen (of whom, in districts with many Clubs, there might be four or five) were incurred for the most part in travelling to the Clubs on official visits; and of these, only one per annum for each Club was paid for specifically by R.I.B.I., the expense of any others falling on the 'Block Grant'.

It was inevitable that, as with all ethical movements subsisting on private subscription and benefaction, varying conceptions of *noblesse oblige* (and varying depths of pocket) determined the extent to which the Block Grant was drawn upon. Rotarians who could afford to do so, and some who could not, systematically refrained from reimbursing themselves for expenses that were sometimes considerable. It was thus equally inevitable, even where *noblesse oblige* might have been overcome by personal need, that some Rotarians were restrained by diffidence and embarrassment, rather than by philanthropy itself, from claiming expenses.

By 1949, the prescribed minimum for Club subscriptions was three guineas a year, of which sum 7s. 6d. went to the support of the 'International's' expenses and 15s. to 'R.I.B.I.' for the general funds of the Movement at home; but there was no maximum—in some Clubs it was six or eight guineas. A sudden decision by all members to draw upon the funds for all expenses would, at almost any time in the history of the Movement, have destroyed its financial balance.

* * * * *

A glance at the map on page 39 will show the comparatively sparse distribution of Clubs in the Districts of Scotland, Wales, and particularly Ireland. The reasons for this are not far to seek. The immense contributions of the Clydeside to heavy industry have fostered the impression among unthinking Sassenachs that Scotland is, throughout its length and breadth, an industrial country. But the Rotary view of a territory is largely geographical, and geographically Scotland is mainly a country of fishermen and crofters, of lowland farms, highland pastures, and small seaside towns.   It has been found that a Rotary Club, if it is to fill the 'classifications' that will support a firm beginning and a prospect of continuity, needs a population basis of at least 5,000.   Small communities such as outlying villages must, even if they manage to form a Club from the available 'classifications', encounter before long the problem of replacing members who die or leave the district; in many of them the 'founder-members' will be irreplaceable, and the Club will collapse.   With these considerations in mind, it is interesting to compare the spread of Rotary in Scotland, over the twenty-five years from 1923 to 1948, with its growth in English Districts which, though smaller, may be comparable in the distribution of their industries.   In 1923 Scotland had eleven Clubs.   So, as it happened, did Districts No. 3 (Northumberland and Durham), No. 6 (Staffordshire, Shropshire, and Warwickshire), and No. 11 (Hampshire and Dorset).   By the end of 1948 Scotland had thirty-eight, and the other three districts had respectively thirty-four, forty-two, and twenty-nine.   These increases are fairly representative of what happened in most Districts over that quarter of a century, and they show Scotland's rate of development to have been normal.   True, there were violent contrasts at the extremes: District No. 10 (Gloucestershire, Somerset, Hereford, and N. Wiltshire) moved only from twenty-two Clubs to twenty-five in that period. District No. 13 (Greater London) leapt from three Clubs to eighty-one, by means of a special technique of 'extension' for which there would have been little scope in Scotland—and less in Ireland and Wales.   But the expansion was otherwise fairly even.

The two districts of North and South Wales presented problems in relation to 'extension' work that were similar to those of Scotland; but whereas in 1923 the North had no Clubs at all and the South had four, twenty-five years later they had sixteen and twenty respectively.   Most of the Clubs are clustered along the northern and southern coastal areas where Welshmen live and work, and while it is doubtful whether the hilly regions of the centre will be capable of development as Rotary centres, the existing Clubs are (generally speaking) small and capable of 'membership expansion' on orthodox lines.

The case of Ireland affords perhaps the clearest illustration of the fact that the Rotary Movement does not depend for its success on numbers.   Ireland was the place of its first settlement on this

A ROTARY DISTRICT MAP
OF
GREAT BRITAIN & IRELAND

Rotary Districts indicated in bold figures and thick lines,
with Counties shown in thin lines.
Smaller figures show the number of Clubs.

1 & 2
(43)

3
(34)

19
(39)

5
(2)

4
(48)

16
(12)

16

5
(49)

7
(43)

18
(29)

6
(45)

8
(32)

15
(22)

13
(82)

10
(26)

9
(32)

14
(52)

12
(35)

11
(24)

17
(23)

11
(5)

11
(2)

side of the Atlantic—the Dublin Club, let us remember, was formed in 1911. Yet by 1923 only two more Clubs had been added—Belfast (also 1911) and Londonderry (1922); and in the ensuing twenty-five years the total had reached only twelve—where it remains today. Nevertheless the Rotary Clubs of Ireland flourished under conditions that were unique in these islands : they survived civil war, partition, republicanism, and irreconcilable religious differences. Indeed, throughout these crises they functioned as pockets of neutrality. During bitter controversies they brought men together in the Clubs and, to the full extent of their passive influence, exploited the non-partisan feelings that all Irishmen held in common.

That Ireland has only twelve clubs to a population of roughly four and a half millions, while Scotland has forty-three to a population of five millions, should be measured against the fact that Scotland has sixty-nine towns with a population exceeding 5,000, while Ireland has only thirty-eight. 'Extension' in Ireland has limits which are more obvious and more daunting than elsewhere. But Irishmen, despite their difficulties, may be said to have shown the way.

*　　*　　*　　*　　*

When the Clubs came to take stock of their position after the Second World War, they saw that a further rapid expansion, even if it were possible, might well produce quantity at the expense of quality. The Clubs had always suffered from constant changes in membership, from wastage due to resignations and deaths and removals and automatic lapsings of 'qualification', sometimes ill-balanced by undiscriminating recruitment. The ideal was a qualitative expansion of the existing Clubs rather than the formation of more and more new ones.

In the provincial Districts this was the attitude to the viviparous breeding of the Clubs that crowded Greater London. The ingenious plan (originating in London in 1933 and adopted by the 'International' at its Convention in St. Louis ten years later) by which a central urban Club relinquished exclusive recruiting rights over a large surrounding territory and 'fathered' the flock of Clubs that grew up on it, was not for them. Outside London, Glasgow alone shared territory with a new Club under this scheme. The Greater London proliferation was attributed (in the provinces) to the fact that in the centre there were twenty-eight Metropolitan Boroughs, each with its Town Hall and municipal entity, and surrounding them a greater number of municipal boroughs and urban district councils representing equally conscious communities, a circumstance which tends to produce its own groupings of trade and professional practice. Only sprawling London could operate such a scheme.

Imperfectly concealed behind this weighty argument lay the fact that a sense of prestige in the large provincial Clubs made them reluctant to encourage upstart rivalry in the neighbourhood. Nevertheless the Clubs of the big cities were themselves much larger than the average of forty members which headquarters thought the desirable figure, and an actual extension of Club membership was doubtfully possible. In 1949, Glasgow had 217 members, Edinburgh 215, Liverpool 207, Birmingham 200, and Manchester 161. (The Rotary Club of London, despite its voluntary sharing of the wider territorial rights, had 254.) But there was no convenient escape from the paradox that there were far more Rotarians per thousand of the population in small towns than in great cities; while in the great cities there were sometimes hundreds of 'classifications' unrepresented in the Clubs. The position is unchanged today.

*   *   *   *   *

It was inevitable that Greater London ('District 13'), with its eighty-odd Clubs placed within easy travelling distance of a central meeting-point, should be closely integrated, powerful, and progressive. The frequent meetings of its District Council sometimes attracted almost 200 men, a fact which, incidentally, precluded any semblance of a 'round table' conference and compelled the use of a platform-and-audience structure; but a certain informality overcame the separatism which this might have caused, and enthusiasm held these large administrative gatherings together. Districts 5 (Lancashire and Cheshire) and 14 (Surrey and West Sussex), with fifty-one Clubs each, had similar difficulties to overcome—and in addition the problem of circuitous railway journeys for some of their Council members. The travel difficulty was more pronounced in District No. 8 (East Anglia), which was notoriously ill-served with cross-country transport. But the Clubs of Scotland, Ireland, and Wales were, by comparison, pockets of isolation. With one District Chairman responsible

D

for the whole of Scotland, and another for the whole of Ireland, Chairmen's visits to Scottish and Irish Clubs were lengthy and onerous undertakings, and District unity suffered in some cases accordingly. These factors, which tended to reduce the self-sufficiency of some of the Districts, must be considered in assessing the Movement of the Districts towards anything resembling autonomy. The strength of the national governing body remained considerable—and, above all, it was the creature of a separate, written Constitution, a circumstance peculiar to the organisation in these islands. In British minds, conditioned by centuries of defiant success in the anomalous practice of government by Crown and Parliament, there would be a predisposition to cherish even a figurehead that had lost all its effective strength. But there were occasions, as we shall see, when the governing body displayed for the benefit of the Districts a strength that was considerably firmer than the tolerated authority of an indulged parent.

Chapter Five

LONDON AND CHICAGO

I

In the nineteen-twenties business men were learning again the bitter lesson which, it now seems, must be learned in each generation that suffers war on the modern scale : the lesson, that is to say, that an apparently crushing indemnity imposed upon a vanquished industrial rival has the opposite effect to that which the victors always intend. The £200,000,000 exacted by Bismarck from a defeated France in the years that followed 1870 were known to have set the French factories humming and French exports booming in a period of prosperity unparalleled in France's history : war reparations must necessarily be made in goods. From 1920 onwards, Germany in her turn had the same experience under the Dawes Plan.

By 1925 it was realized that she had borrowed so freely abroad, and that American and British investors had been such willing lenders at 8 per cent on long term, that she had accumulated debts to about twice the amount she had paid in reparations. In other words, she had not paid reparations, but borrowed them. German exports were nevertheless mounting rapidly, the German standard of living was improving—and the Rotary Movement had taken root and was spreading vigorously throughout the Reich.

Meanwhile Britain's vast war debt to the United States, the liquidation of which had not yet reached the stage at which annual 'token payments' were to prepare the way for cancellation, was already embarrassing the friends of Anglo-American understanding on both sides of the Atlantic. 'They hired the money, didn't they ? ' President Coolidge had said. And many Englishmen were ashamed that their national finances should place them in the position of hopeless debtors because they were already, vis-à-vis half the nations of the Old World, hopeless creditors.

On those higher levels which achieve all the publicity, therefore, Anglo-American relations were not happy; and a reflected unhappiness is discernible in the speeches then being made at Rotary Conferences in this country by business men to whom the position was becoming rapidly clearer and the prospects of world unity darker.

Rotarians are not pessimists. Their Movement is itself an expression of optimism and a declaration that the world's perplexities are capable of solution by resolute men. They found unexpected support in the carefully stated belief of John Maynard Keynes (*The End of Laissez-Faire*, 1926) that there was ' a potency for good in the money-making and money-loving instincts of individuals '; a belief which, Keynes declared, would always stand in the way of his becoming a Socialist. But he saw and announced that the day of collective action was fast approaching, and that it would ' improve the technique of capitalism '.

Winston Churchill had, as Chancellor of the Exchequer, shocked orthodox economists by restoring the Gold Standard in 1925. The staple industries, iron and steel, cotton, coal, and wool, were entering the stage of deep depression which was to be deepened by the great ' economic blizzard ' of 1929–31. Hundreds of idle cotton-mills were in the hands of creditors. Every coalfield took advantage of the Coal Mines Act of 1926, extending the time for which workers could remain underground, and many mines had re-introduced the eight-hour day and lower wages. The arrival of ' reparation ' coal from Germany was responsible, among other causes, for the closing of hundreds of pits, and by 1927 the weekly output in Britain's key industry had fallen to 4,700,000 tons, against a potential capacity of 6,200,000. This catastrophic fall had brought about, in 1926, a lock-out in the coal industry that precipitated a General Strike and brought the country face to face with the urgent need for a new alignment of capital and labour, on the basis that all were ' in it together '.

The General Council of the Trades Union Congress, which had called the General Strike, accepted an invitation from Sir Alfred Mond and twenty-five industrialists to a conference, to discuss ' means for raising the efficiency of industry and improving the workers' standards of living '. Views expressed at that conference echoed the statements on trade relationships that had been made at Rotary conferences for years past, and were to receive striking confirmation in 1946, when the Rotary Clubs of Great

Britain and Ireland combined in an industrial survey [1] of out-
standing value on the theme of co-operation between employers
and men. It is perhaps the main significance of the Rotary
Movement that its members, as representatives of businesses still
small enough to reflect personal relationships, understand and
sympathize with their employees in a way that the combines and
cartels cannot.

In 1927, when Rotary in Great Britain was to revive the
question of its relationship with Rotary International at a world
Convention in Ostend, it seemed that a period of recuperation
was about to follow the unprecedented labour crisis of 1926;
and it was thought that the out-and-out ' economic nationalism '
which was threatening Anglo-American relations more seriously
than ever might be averted, after all. There was much to foster
this illusion. A world economic conference convened by the
League of Nations was about to meet at Geneva—one of the
British delegates was Sydney Pascall of the London Rotary Club,
who was to be the first European to become President of Rotary
International and who successfully enlisted the League of Nations'
interest in a campaign against bribery in commerce and industry.
Keynes's prophecy about collective action in the capitalist world
appeared to be coming true, though it was watched without
enthusiasm by the T.U.C. Amalgamation movements in industry
were in full swing. The armaments-making, shipbuilding, and
steel businesses of Armstrong's and Vickers' became Vickers-
Armstrongs Ltd. Debenhams' joined the Drapery Trust which
controlled the majority of the big provincial drapery stores.
1927 also saw the fusion of Anton Jurgen's and Van den Bergh's,
the two largest margarine manufacturers and provision-shop
owners in Europe. Selfridge's amalgamated with Whiteley's.
The Lancashire and Yorkshire Bank joined the Bank of Liverpool
and Martin's under the name of Martin's Bank. But these fusions
of once-competitive interests were defensive and, on the whole,
they proved inimical to the capital-labour *rapprochement* started by
Sir Alfred Mond and his supporters after the General Strike.

There was an appearance of prosperity. Although the National
Debt stood at over seven thousand millions, a series of gigantic
conversion operations by the Treasury were well supported by
the holders of Government Stock—and set the pattern for a kind

[1] *Combined Operations.* R.I.B.I. Pamphlet No. 16.

of budget-balancing that was to become familiar. Capital issues were greater than in any year since the war.

All these large-scale financial manipulations tended, as should perhaps have been expected, to alienate still further the working from the employing class; and it was left to the smaller business men, among whom most British Rotarians are to be found, to work out a *modus vivendi*. As costs in business rose so high that competition became difficult, it was easier for the big bosses to negotiate price-rings and cartels, or to lobby for protective tariffs, than to replan their businesses on productive lines. The smaller business men, seeing this happen, were antagonized and drew closer to the workers. The Rotarian's ideal of 'service above self' became more and more the ideal of the small business man. It was at no time the battle-cry of what has been called the 'managerial revolution'; it was not the mainspring of the industrial trusts and combines. Rotarian literature of the time shows that the Clubs (as will be described in Chapter Six) were deeply and unhappily aware of the mounting tragedy of unemployment, and were turning their energies to numerous schemes—of varying efficacy—for its alleviation.

It may be [H. G. Wells had just written in the concluding chapter of his *Outline of History*] that private enterprise will refuse to learn the lesson of Service without some quite catastrophic revolution. We do not know; we cannot tell. These are unnecessary disasters, but they may be unavoidable disasters. Human history becomes more and more a race between education and catastrophe.

*　　　*　　　*　　　*　　　*

II

The story of Rotary Clubs, the description of their complicated allegiance to Rotary International, to headquarters at 'national' level, to the chairmen and councils of their Districts, and even to the bond of union within each club itself, is a story of written and re-written Constitutions, of tortuously-worded amendments, the dotting of i's and the crossing of t's. It is, indeed, a strange story of tradition-loving Britons caught up in the endless process of justifying their traditions on paper. The Annual Conference, discussed as a piece of machinery in Chapter Thirteen, is the perennial target of much legislative effort, varying greatly in its aptitude for self-expression and reflecting often the work of Club members in the legal professions. ' Plain men ' in the Movement, impatient of verbal niceties and the unavoidable pomposity of restraint by declaration, call it ' tinkering with the Constitution '. Theirs is the insularity of secure centuries, the habit of *laissez-faire* that erects common and tacit consent into a system and calls it an ' unwritten constitution ', England's gift to the world. But Rotary came from America, where the art of constitution-writing, owing much to Rousseau and more to the determination of the Colonists to know where they stood for the future, has reached its final, rigid perfection. ' Rotary ', accordingly, is a prescription rather than a tradition.

From 1914 to 1920 the British Clubs had developed to some extent along their own lines, as did the ' British Association of Rotary Clubs ' which was formed in 1914. But in 1921, when that Association embodied forty-eight clubs and its headquarters had moved from Edinburgh to London, Rotary International held its annual Convention at Edinburgh (the Convention's first visit to Europe), and a movement towards greater unity took place. The British Association of Rotary Clubs changed its name, and indeed its status, by becoming ' Rotary International : Association for Great Britain and Ireland ' (a title later changed for the only less cumbersome one of ' Rotary International in Great Britain and Ireland ') : but it insisted on certain ' terms of union ' that were to preserve the autonomy it had enjoyed during the comparative isolation of the war years. These ' terms of union ' were given expression in seven Principles. They are quoted here because they aptly summarize the relationship which, though it was not destined to last more than five years, was then established as a working compromise :

1. That in any plan devised for the government of Rotary, the Rotary Clubs throughout the world should not be asked to surrender their direct membership in an international association.
2. That such international association shall be entrusted with the preservation and development of the fundamentals of Rotary, including its ideals, its ethics, its emblem, and its unique features of organisation.
3. That such international association shall continue to hold an annual Convention.
4. That nothing in the Constitution of such international association

shall prevent the fullest control being granted to the Rotary Clubs of each nation over all matters which are exceptionally national in their scope.

5. That all national organizations which may be devised shall have power to organize, administer and give national expression to the Rotary movement within their respective territories.

6. That the activities and powers of such national organizations should be so co-ordinated with the activity and powers of the international association as to secure the union and harmonious working of Rotary institutions throughout the world; and in particular that the governing body of the international association be made up from persons comprising the governing bodies of the various national associations so far as may be possible.

7. That to the British Association of Rotary Clubs should be ceded the same powers as they now have under their present organisation, so far as is compatible with the principles of the International Association enunciated in the foregoing paragraphs.

When the International Association of Rotary Clubs had re-christened itself 'Rotary International', and issued as such its first Constitution (1922), those seven principles were agreed to have been duly embodied. The new Constitution provided for a regionalized form of supervision—

through one of the following forms of administration, namely

    (a) National or territorial administration

or (b) District administration under direct supervision of Rotary International.

In 1927, however, the International took notice of the fact that no countries other than Great Britain and Ireland had, in fact, adopted a 'national or territorial administration' for their associated clubs. It decided that the British, with their semi-autonomous administration, had made it appear that there was a 'duality of control'; possibilities of discord and misunderstanding were said to flow from this, and the International re-opened a contentious question by proposing a system of controlled 'areas', aggregations of 'Districts' (there are now eighteen in Great Britain) working under the Area Councils. An Area Council would be composed of the 'District Governors'.

Now, Great Britain and Ireland had never adopted the American system of placing each Rotary 'District' under a Governor. Here, the 'Districts' of Rotary were (and are) administered by

District Councils, each representing from twelve to more than eighty Clubs, and comprising sometimes over 100 men sharing the responsibility of the ' District '—as compared with the American District Governor, who was solely responsible, as an individual, to Chicago. (Today he may appoint his own advisory committee if he likes, but it is allowed no responsibility.) In 1938, the position arose that every ' District ' in this country had a ' District Chairman ', as well as a ' Representative Member '. The former, elected locally, was *ex officio* a member of the General Council (the governing body of the Association). The latter, though nominated locally, was elected at the International Convention, and thus owed his office to the votes of Rotarians from all parts of the world. Which of these two officers in each ' District ' was eligible to attend the Convention, involving that most coveted prize of office—a free trip to America ? For the purposes of the Convention, one or other of them was admittedly superfluous; but there was a difference of view between London and Chicago as to which one it was. Chicago gracefully compromised by inviting them both, a gesture that must have added some thousands of pounds to the cost borne that year by the ' International '. The following year, ' R.I.B.I.' decided to merge the two offices in the person of the District Chairman, who was thereafter the ' Rotary International Representative ' as well as a member of the General Council in this country. There were other minor concessions of principle or administration on both sides; but the fundamental differences survived.

The earlier differences had, indeed, been emphasized rather than settled by the ' R.I.B.I.' Constitution agreed upon in 1924. Article II of that Constitution defined the purpose of the Association in this country as follows :

1. To promote *in the area* (i.e. in Great Britain and Ireland) the fundamental principles and objects of Rotary as laid down by Rotary International.
2. To co-ordinate the methods and activities of Rotary Clubs *in the Area*, and to organize new clubs therein.
3. To collect all necessary information, and to distribute it in such ways as may, *in the judgement of the Association*, best advance the Rotary movement.
4. To promote the spirit of fraternity and harmony amongst Rotary Clubs and their members, and to co-operate in all possible ways

in the extension and development of Rotary throughout the world.

The corresponding article of the Constitution of Rotary International says merely this :

(a) To encourage, promote, extend and supervise Rotary throughout the world;
(b) To co-ordinate and generally direct the activities of Rotary International.

One of Rotary's pioneers in this country, C. E. White of Belfast, was chairman of the Committee which drafted the 1924 Constitution for Great Britain and Ireland. At the Association's Annual Conference at Torquay in 1924 he was asked by a delegate why the purposes of the two Constitutions should be different. His reply from the platform expresses exactly the feeling of British ' Rotary ' at that time—and indeed the feeling of many Rotarians today—on the difficult question of Chicago authority. ' I want to answer that question now,' he said. ' If the objects of R.I.B.I. were the same as those of Rotary International, there would be no need for us to be a separate territorial unit. Those of you who came into the Movement before the Edinburgh Conference will remember the discussion insisting on certain rights, without which we would not give up our name, " British Association of Rotary Clubs ", and adopt " Rotary International ". There were certain clauses agreed to, that we should have certain rights if we became a territorial unit in Rotary International; the right of self-government, the right of appointing our own secretary, what literature should come across the Atlantic into our islands, the right to send out literature from our own headquarters, instead of its coming from Rotary International headquarters. You will see, therefore, that Article II forms the Magna Charta of British Rotary. It contains the rights and privileges we possess, and it is put there for the benefit of Rotary as a whole. Though our aims are the same as those of Rotary International, it is recognized by us that the great objective of Rotary International, as expressed in the words " the advancement of understanding, goodwill, and international peace through a world fellowship of business and professional men united in the ideal of service ", will be best preserved and fostered by the elimination of friction, *which might arise through the differing expressions, customs, and coinage in these islands compared with those of America and Canada.'*

So it was a difference of vernacular, and behaviour, and national awareness, and the metric system ? More probably it was a difference too deep and subtle for analysis or definition, a traditional difference of the kind that British imperialism has grown to recognize and respect in the peoples of the Commonwealth. If the Governing body of Rotary International had been members of a race of successful colonial administrators, with a genius for the haphazard creation of voluntary loyalties, they might have evolved a Rotary ' Statute of Westminster ', binding the whole international structure to Chicago as the British Commonwealth freely binds itself to the Crown. Or they might not. The British, perhaps, are a cocky race, conditioned by centuries to think that the phrase ' Britons never shall be slaves ' means that Britain shall always be top dog. Speculation lies outside the scope of this book : but in the crucial struggle for survival as a major economic Power that lies ahead for this country, the relationships of ' R.I.' and ' R.I.B.I.' may well serve as a microcosm of the larger confrontation of Britain and the U.S.A.

* * * * *

The Resolution by which, in 1927, Rotary in Great Britain formally declared its readiness to take its full place in the ' International ' fold after ensuring that a number of hurdles would be missing from the stockade, was submitted at an International Convention, the ' supreme court ' of Rotary, meeting this time at Ostend. Its language is so exactly typical of the forensic solemnity of ' Rotary ' resolutions, and it is at the same time so important a milestone in the development of ' Rotary ' in this country, that it is given here in full. It was in effect a proposal to support a similar, though less guarded, resolution tabled by the ' International '.

Whereas the supreme object of the Rotary Movement is to advance understanding, goodwill and international peace, through a world fellowship of business and professional men united in the ideal of service;

Whereas in order to advance that object there is need for harmony in the relationships of clubs, districts, and areas [1] with each other, and

---

[1] Great Britain and Ireland is an ' area '.

together with the administrative body of the whole movement, i.e. the Board of Rotary International;

Whereas the Constitution provides for the setting up of various forms of subordinate administration, including ' National or Territorial Units ', of which only one is at present duly constituted;

Whereas the existence of only one ' National' unit in an International Movement presents the appearance of duality and the possibility of lack of harmony and understanding;

It is resolved by this Eighth Conference of Rotary International: Association for Great Britain and Ireland,

That support be given to Resolution No. 3 tabled by the Board of Rotary International providing for the establishment of Area Administrations, and that in the event of the passing of such resolution the Board of R.I.B.I. be recommended to take the necessary steps to submit to the Board of Rotary International proposals applying for an Area Administration with Rules of Procedure which shall have powers to control local finances, to convene Conferences and Assemblies, to appoint Committees, to give local expression to programmes, set up a Headquarters and Staff, conduct a periodical or bulletin, and generally to promote in the area the fundamental principles and objects of Rotary and advise concerning special ways and means of carrying them into effect.

By this instrument British Rotarians contrived to present an appearance of anxiety to re-enter the international fold while making it clear that Rotary ideals must remain subject to national interpretation and practice. Speakers at British meetings, indeed, took occasion to commend the scheme to Rotarians on grounds which other speakers suspected as rationalizations. 'Its birth,' said Sydney Pascall (then President of R.I.B.I.) at the 1927 Conference, ' is due to two things. In the first place the demand in parts of the European continent for a local expression of their point of view, a local expression of Rotarianism as it appeals to their Continental national character. Secondly, a feeling that British Rotary, R.I.B.I., has never quite filled its part of the main stream of Rotary International. . . . We do feel that there is something more to be gained through linking us into the real international organization; and it is for those two reasons that this area scheme has seen the light. The scheme is an attempt for the first time to free the Board of Rotary International from purely local affairs and administration. This is the question : can we do something to make Rotary International a true international organization ? *This, through inevitable facts of birth and development, it has hitherto not been, but it is what, to achieve its greatest possibilities, it must become.'*

Pascall was supported by Canon W. Thompson Elliott, of the Leeds Rotary Club, President of ' R.I.B.I.' in 1924, who described ' the growing recognition that some devolution of administration from the headquarters in Chicago had become necessary '. He mentioned that the Board of Rotary International sat for five days at a time; ' and of those five days ', he said, ' three days are taken up with the discussion of details of administration which ought to be devolved from that Board to a lesser authority. The Board has not got the time to concentrate its attention on the international problems which I think it should exist for.'

But from Ireland came hard-headed scepticism and opposition. ' Is it likely,' demanded W. H. Alexander, of the Belfast Club, ' that if we gave up our autonomy there would be more harmony ? Rotary was formed in this country in 1914 without any assistance from Rotary International. . . . I think instead of abolishing the only territorial unit we have in existence, we should ask Rotary International to go on and form more in Europe.' W. A. McConnell, another of the Movement's pioneers, representing the Dublin Club, then told the Conference that they were ' tinkering with the Constitution ', a phrase destined to be used by the opponents of change at every annual Conference thereafter. ' I can't understand,' he said, with a logical frankness that was to go unanswered, ' the idea of making an application for an Area Administration if you are told that it does not bind you. The proper thing would be to know the proper lines upon which you would like that area administration to be given to you, and if Rotary International were prepared to give you those lines you would make up your mind on the matter.'

*   *   *   *   *

The British Clubs decided to support the proposed change. Their decision was later said to have been due to a belief that it would entail no more than a common dedication to ideals, with a continued separation of control over international and ' area ' finance. This idea was strengthened by the fact that the scheme's endorsement by the 1927 Convention at Ostend, though only provisional, had been accompanied by whole-hearted acceptance of the British ' aims and objects ' plan (see Chapter Six), the greatest integrating force which the world Movement had yet encountered. Rotarians then discovered the Fabian principle of handing controversies to 'expert' commissions of enquiry, plus the time-honoured British legislative custom of rejecting the commission's long-awaited recommendations. It was not until 1931 that a form of Constitution providing for separate 'area administrations' was agreed upon by the experts from both sides of the Atlantic—and then the British Movement turned it down at its Annual Conference at Llandudno, on the ground that 'all real control, including that of finance', would be vested by it in Chicago, and that this would mean the total destruction of local autonomy. An international commission then took up the problem (the 'Commission on Rotary International Administration'), and in due course presented a report that sought to balance the views of the contenders.

The seven Rotary personalities who comprised this Commission came respectively from England, New York, Kentucky, Newfoundland, Sweden, Madras and Uruguay. They wrestled for three years with the problem of so reshaping the International Constitution (which it was deemed impossible to rewrite completely) as to embrace and 'legalize' all the purely national characteristics that had attached themselves to the Movement as it spread across the world. In particular they sought a compromise that could embody *in the Constitution* the 'territorial unit' status of the special organization in Great Britain and Ireland. (In their global journeyings to meet and deliberate they cost the 'International' twenty thousand dollars.) They produced in 1937 a voluminous report, including a masterly summary of 'the Present Organisation and Structure of R.I. and Historical Background', which must long remain an unimpeachable source-book of Rotary history. They proposed the adoption of a form of 'regional administration' which they thought would solve (among others) the main problem this chapter has discussed; and they were prepared, if given time, to complete their work by drafting the highly complicated 'legislation' that this would entail.

But at the International Convention at Nice in 1937, after a prolonged and sometimes heated discussion, the 'Commission of Seven' was thanked and disbanded.

At the same time, it was decided that the 'Board of Directors'

governing the Association in this country should become its
'General Council', composed mainly of the District Chairmen—
who at the same time became the Association's delegates to the
International Conventions. And the following year, at San
Francisco, the Convention confirmed a British proposal that the
'Districts of R.I.B.I.' should in future be Districts of the International itself, as the Clubs were already member-clubs of the
International itself. These acts of assimilation to the International were at the same time symbolized by a change of name
from *Rotary International : Association for Great Britain and Ireland*
to *Rotary International in Great Britain and Ireland*. The word 'in'
was felt to be newly and happily significant.

But although these steps brought 'R.I.B.I.' considerably closer
to the International, they left the main problem of its constitutional position unresolved. That, the 1937 Convention had said
(the British delegates dissenting), could be left to the legislative
resources of succeeding Conventions; and even this involved
an assumption which only a few were prepared to make, namely
that the problem was capable of solution at all. The Munich
crisis in European affairs and the six years of war that followed it
defeated any such intentions; and the anomalous 'constitutional'
position of 'R.I.B.I.' remains the same today as it has been for
over twenty years.

How may that position be summarized? Here, at least, is an
attempt. In 1922, at Los Angeles, 'R.I.B.I.' was granted
recognition as a 'territorial unit', with qualified powers of self-
government. In 1927, at Ostend, all 'territorial units' were
abolished in favour of a new 'area administration' Resolution
which somewhat enhanced the authority of the 'International';
but this Resolution carried a proviso that preserved the British
status (and only the British status) as a 'territorial unit' on the old
basis. It was, and it remains, a Resolution of the Convention—
it has never found its way into the Constitution; and R.I.B.I.
continued to exist, therefore, as a kind of excrescence on the
International Constitution, nourished by a subordinate piece of
legislation that has never yet been made substantive. In 1930,
at Chicago, a new and tighter plan of 'area administration' was
produced, in the hope that R.I.B.I. might come in under it.
R.I.B.I. rejected it. In 1934, at Detroit, all 'area administration'
schemes were (almost in exasperation) abolished—but the Resolu-

tion of 1927, whose proviso was still keeping R.I.B.I. precariously alive, was left untouched, and the 'Commission of Seven' was launched on its quest for the perfect solution—with the inconclusive result already described.

The war over, British *laissez faire* might have let this situation go on indefinitely. To the Briton who thinks about it at all, the word 'Constitution' itself has come to epitomize a mass of contradictions. 'A rigid Constitution,' James Bryce declared, 'necessarily represents the past, not the present.' But the question was international, as international as U.N.O. or the Red Cross. A solution must be found. When this book went to press the search for it was still engaging the attention of a handful of puzzled men, while the main body of Rotarians in Great Britain and Ireland, in blissful unawareness of their equivocal state, paid their dues to Chicago and got on with the business of being Rotarians.

*　　　*　　　*　　　*　　　*

Chapter Six

COMMUNITY OF PURPOSE

' I PREFER association to gregariousness,' wrote Benjamin Disraeli.
' It is a community of purpose that constitutes society.' Community proceeds from the readiness of individuals to forswear
personal predilections and, as with members of a political party,
to sink differences in order to go forward on matters agreed upon.
In the mid-nineteen twenties the Rotary Clubs of this country
were still strongly individualistic in their interpretation of the
' Objects of Rotary ' (see page 5). To the majority of members,
the ' development of acquaintance as an opportunity for service '
was no more than a frequent, regular, and amiable getting
together to see what could be done—by the enthusiasts. ' High
ethical standards in business ' was a term of limitless scope,
lending itself to countless subjective variations in meaning; if
some rationally unavoidable forms of business chicanery might be
held ' higher ' than others, that at least gave them an altitude of
some sort. Rotarians were uneasy about this. Guy Gundaker
of Philadelphia, President of the ' International ' in 1924, told the
British conference of that year that ' it requires hard thinking to
decide whether a business action is right or wrong '. He discussed some trade customs, especially the misnaming of articles
of food on a bill of fare. ' For instance,' he said, ' there is York
Ham. If all the ham designated York Ham came from Yorkshire,
that shire must have only one industry—pig-raising. In America
all bills of fare contain fillet of sole. Now sole is a fish indigenous
to England . . . this misnaming is a trade custom.' Three years
later, at a conference of Rotary club secretaries, an accountant
startled his audience by asking : ' Do we, as Rotarians, sufficiently
investigate the companies and the shares we hold as investors ?
Do we see that the conditions of employment that our money is
helping are ethical ? ' He went unanswered; ' ethical ' conditions of employment carried too many definitions.

' The recognition of the worthiness of all useful occupa-

E

tions . . . ? ' There were Rotarians who felt this to be a prig's
counsel of perfection. (There still are.) They professed to see
its aptest expression in the Cecil Alexander hymn of the 1880's :

> The rich man in his castle,
> The poor man at his gate,
> God made them, high or lowly,
> And ordered their estate.

' Worthiness,' they said, was the language of facile *ex parte* judgement—unless it was to be applied solely to the occupations which
qualified for Rotary membership. In relation to some of the more
sordid jobs remaining to be done by the ' proletariat ', words
such as these stuck in the throats of men who had set Ruskin's
Dignity of Labour against the mocking background of industrialism.

On the other hand, ' the dignifying by each Rotarian of *his*
occupation as an opportunity to serve society ' was seen by many
as Rotary's grandest conception. And again, it still is. ' Every
person who lives by any useful work,' said John Stuart Mill,
' should be habituated to regard himself, not as an individual
working for his private benefit but as a public functionary.'
A Rotarian today would applaud this as ' good Rotary '. But
he would only partially agree with Henry Sidgwick's comment,
in his *Elements of Politics*, that ' it is the business of the moralist
and the preacher, not of the legislator, to aim at producing in the
community this habit of thought and feeling '. Rotarians saw a
better way of working towards ultimate good than either of these.
One of their declared objects transcended both legislator and
preacher. It was ' the application of the ideal of service by every
Rotarian to his personal, business and community life '.

In this, however, lay the greatest scope for diversity of action;
and although there were attempts at co-ordination within the
Clubs, many of which had split themselves into numerous committees charged with this and that aspect of ' service ', there was
little uniformity among the Clubs as a whole. To a lesser extent
this was true also of their undertaking to ' encourage and foster
the advancement of international understanding, goodwill, and
peace through a world fellowship of business and professional
men united in the ideal of service '. This was then their ' Sixth
Object ' (it is now, by re-drafting, their fourth and last); and such
uniformity of ' international ' Club action as there was could have

been attributed to the fact that, since few of the Clubs knew what they could do to 'foster international peace', comparatively little was being done.

*　　*　　*　　*　　*

In 1927, Rotarians in Britain were becoming more aware of the international character of their Movement. In this awareness they were, perhaps, led by Sydney Pascall, whose trade relationships as well as his Rotary interests were international in scope; and it was Pascall who, with two like-minded colleagues in the Movement, devised a scheme for the ' rationalization ' of Rotary objectives that was to win international approval. The other two men were Vivian Carter, then general secretary of ' R.I.B.I.' and editor of the *Rotary Wheel*, and William Moffat, a Shetlands man belonging to the Leeds Club, an insurance manager by occupation, and a man with the particular gift of lucid exposition that was needed to explain the scheme to the Clubs.

The authors of the ' Aims and Objects Plan', as it was called, did not claim to be the recipients of a vision. In a period when the word had not yet acquired its modern opprobrium, they were planners. Every Rotarian knew that his Club was required to be more than a luncheon Club (even if some Clubs were very little more). Most of them knew that spasmodic acts of charity were not ' Rotary ', though they would insist (and will still insist) on their right to give money or goods to causes that touch the springs of charity. All of them knew that their acts of ' service ' rested on the goodwill of the individual. But the thinking men in the Movement saw that, because the declared *Objects of Rotary* were vague and unspecific, the leadership of the Movement was hamstrung. The common denominator of those ' Objects ', however, was ' service '; and on examination they seemed to fall into four groups or forms of expression. Running a healthy Club was in itself the foundation of the Movement : it should be known as ' Club Service '. The job of honest broker was the Rotarian's main dedication : it should be called ' Vocational Service '. Social alleviations and cultural work should be grouped as a separate activity : let it be named ' Community Service '. And the use of the Movement to promote (through the action of individuals) the comity of nations, and liberate men from the crippling fear of war, came (a year later) to be called ' International Service '.

Every Club was to have four committees bearing these names. Every 'District' in Great Britain was to have four similar committees. 'R.I.B.I.' would itself have four such committees—and, in due course, the four were reflected in the organization of Rotary International at Chicago. In Chicago and London, at District level, and in the larger Clubs, there would be an 'Aims and Objects Committee' to co-ordinate the work of the other four. (In smaller Clubs, and Clubs which chose to regard an 'Aims and Objects Committee' as superfluous, this would be done by the Club Council.)

'This scheme,' Moffat told a conference of club secretaries in 1927, 'is really a simplification . . . because it looks at Rotary from the three fundamental principles of the man's Club, the man's job, and the man as citizen.' It was simple enough seen from the top of the administrative ladder, but it was a more drastic simplification for Clubs which had arranged themselves in as many as twenty-five committees than it was for those Clubs that had drifted happily along with no committees at all. Moreover, it proposed (though it avowedly did no more than propose) that the Club Service Committee in every Club should appoint no fewer than ten sub-committees to deal with the essentials of Club organization. (These are reviewed in Chapter Seven.) The other committees—Vocational, Community, and International— were felt to be indivisible units, to each of which the numerous aspects of its work would present unifying similarities. A typical plan of the committee organization in a medium sized Club is reproduced on page 61.

*　　　*　　　*　　　*　　　*

The strength of the scheme was its provision of 'lines of communication' from top to bottom of the Movement. The organization came alive. Successive Presidents, in consultation with the Association's paid secretariat, evolved elaborations of 'reporting' procedure that led to a multiplicity of ruled and printed forms of distinctive colours. Every committee was supposed to report to its namesake, on the way up to the hierarchy, as to the work it had been doing during a stated period. In a voluntary organization lacking corrective sanctions for the dilatory, these reports varied enormously in usefulness and intelligibility. In some of the Clubs—and even some of the 'Districts '—

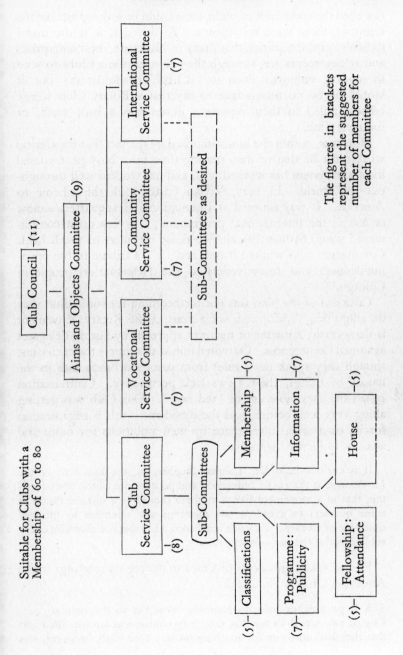

Suitable for Clubs with a Membership of 60 to 80

Club Council —(11)

Aims and Objects Committee —(9)

Vocational Service Committee —(7)

Community Service Committee —(7)

International Service Committee —(7)

Sub-Committees as desired

Club Service Committee —(8)

Sub-Committees

Classifications —(5)

Membership —(5)

Programme: Publicity —(7)

Information —(7)

Fellowship: Attendance —(5)

House —(5)

The figures in brackets represent the suggested number of members for each Committee not even the complaint of uselessness could be levelled against the reports : there were no reports. To this day, it is the major difficulty of the historian that many of ' Rotary's ' best enterprises and achievements are, through the failure of some Clubs to send in reports, unknown even to ' R.I.B.I.' headquarters; but it would be by no means true to say that a Rotary Club whose officers failed in their reporting duties was a bad, weak, or indolent Club.

However, within the limits imposed by the fact that the clerical work must be that of men sparing time from busy professional lives, the system has worked well, and has worked well throughout the world. In 1927, Vivian Carter took the scheme to America. It was adopted at International Headquarters almost *en bloc* as the international programme; ' a very great compliment,' wrote Sydney Pascall, ' to those members of the R.I.B.I. Committees who worked it out, and . . . a tribute to the openmindedness and receptiveness of the Headquarters people in Chicago.'

Criticism of the plan was not forthcoming for some time after its adoption. ' Adoption ' of a plan in the Rotary Movement is democratic, a matter of majority approval by voting delegates at annual Conferences. Outvoted minorities supply the criticisms, though they speak (as a rule) from parochial briefs and, in the nature of things, their views lack perspective. Centralization raised the inevitable cry of ' red tape '. Our Club was getting along very well before, said the dissidents : this is organization for its own sake, interference by men ambitious for office and anxious to justify themselves.

It is curious [said Dr. Thomas Stephenson, the President of the Movement, at the 1928 Conference] and perhaps not a little disconcerting, that in a movement like ours there should be a distinct desire in some quarters to avoid at our meetings any reference to the real objective of Rotary. At Club luncheons addresses are given on every subject under the sun—except Rotary. . . .

He had asked presidents of Clubs to devote six meetings to the Aims and Objects Plan.

A large number paid no attention whatever to the request. . . . One or two wrote to say that their programme was already filled and that they had no room for anything more. One Club, however, was perfectly frank. The President replied saying he feared it wouldn't be possible to carry out the programme suggested because his members were not interested in Rotary !

The transformation of the mere ' luncheon clubs ' into the new-model Rotary Clubs was a skilful and patient process of ' education ' and the constant changing of responsible personnel. Two or three Clubs died ' on their feet ', and their charters were withdrawn. To this day it is possible to encounter Rotary Clubs with no committees at all and Rotarians who do not know what committees there are supposed to be. But on the whole the committee structure is firmly established, and its chief critics are those who deprecate their multiplicity. (' Rotary is in danger of being enslaved by the elaborately-organized committee system,' a university professor told the Exeter Club as recently as 1945.) In the next four chapters the work of Rotary Clubs through that system from 1927 onwards is illustrated and examined.

Chapter Seven

'CLUB SERVICE'

EVERY Rotary Club had (or was presumed to have) its Club
Council, comprising the Club's President for the year, its Immediate Past-President, one or more appointed Vice-Presidents, the
treasurer, the secretary and six ordinary members who are elected
by ballot.   It met once a month (or oftener if it wished); and its
duties were described as ' administrative rather than inspirational '
—it was concerned, that is to say, with the mechanics rather
than the ethics of the Club.   But unless there was also an ' Aims
and Objects Committee ' (as there was in the larger Clubs) it
received the reports of the four committees dealing with Club,
Vocational, Community, and International Service.   In a small
Club the chairmen of those Committees were usually members of
the Club Council.

In its new emphasis on ' Service ', the ' Aims and Objects plan '
involved the conception of sound Club organization as one form
of Rotarian service to the public.   Those who served on Club
Service Committees were doing an act of service no less valuable
than those who, under other Committees, went in for social service
outside the Club.   In many Clubs, indeed, they necessarily
worked considerably harder.   Their terms of reference gave them
the responsibility of organizing all the internal life and activities
of the Club and its social relations with other Rotary Clubs,
subject to the control of the Club Council.   Until a Club was fully
organized and established they were regarded as the most important of all the Committees; and at all times they co-ordinated the
work of a larger number of subsidiary committees than any other.

Ten of these subsidiary Committees were contemplated by the
' Aims and Objects Plan '.   Their functions were as follows :

Classifications.   To survey all the businesses and professions carried
on in the Club's territory, keep a list of those that were represented in
the Club and those that were not, and revise them (where constitu-
tionally possible) to get the desired men into the Club.

This was to be a small committee—two or three men with special local knowledge. It worked by the rubric of the Outline of Classifications (see page 23), which at that time had no Anglicized supplement, and might require the identification of an English poultry-farmer with an industry described as ' duck-raising ' or place the owner of a window-cleaning business under ' Laundering, Cleaning, and Dyeing '. No ' Major Classification ' (a group heading covering all the branches of an industry) should normally contain more than 10 per cent of the Club's total membership; and no one was to be considered eligible for membership unless he spent at least 60 per cent of his business time and activity within the territory of the Club. The classifications were set under three main headings—manufacturing, distributing, retailing—though there were certain professions that fell within none of them and had to be specially provided for. This whole question of finding classifications for desirable members (which still, in some of the Clubs, attracts more enthusiasm and ingenuity than finding members to fill vacant classifications) had some growing pains : the printed lists came under constant revision as this or that vocation, peculiar perhaps to this country, was found to have been omitted from the American list in universal use (pawnbroking was an example). Duplications were frequent, naïve, ingenious, and artful. ' If they want you in a Rotary Club,' people said, ' they'll find a classification for you even if it's supposed to be filled already.' The Chairman of the R.I.B.I. ' Classifications Committee ' told the secretaries' conference in 1927 that he knew of a Club that contained five solicitors, one of whom was classified as a Pier Manager.

One step that put Rotary on a slightly different footing from other ' classification club ' movements was the admission of ' associate members '. This was a considerable modification of Rotary's claim to be based on the ' single classification ' principle, though it had been in operation in Rotary Clubs outside Great Britain and Ireland for some years before it was adopted here. The 1924 edition of the International ' By-laws ' said that any member could nominate for ' associate membership ' one partner, officer, or other responsible person ' actively connected with the company or firm he represents '. An associate member had no vote and could not hold any Club office; and he ceased to be a member at all if he or his nominator left the firm, or if the latter died or left the Club. The idea was American, and by 1929 it had grown into a system of admitting ' additional active members ' (the original ' associate members ', but with powers to vote and hold office). But in that year it was rejected by the British Conference on the grounds that it would weaken the sense of individual responsibility, introduce the very inhibitions between ' two of a trade ' that Paul Harris had wished to exclude, and make the Clubs unwieldy, ill-balanced, and numerically difficult to accommodate for luncheons. The ' additional active member ' was not admitted to British Clubs until 1933, by which time there were also ' past service membership ' (for previous ' active ' members who had retired from business), honorary membership for ' men who have distinguished themselves by meritorious service in the furtherance of Rotary ideals ', and (later) ' senior active membership ' for ' active ' members of long service and men who had held high office in the Movement. A further exception was made in the case of Press representatives, ' more than one ' paper in the Club's territory being allowed to have a member in the Club. This set no limit to the number of Pressmen who could join one Club (other than the number of local papers), and was a clear recognition not merely that publicity was important but that it should be purveyed by initiates.

*   *   *   *   *

Membership. To ' vet ' proposals for new membership, from what was tactfully called the ' personal side '.

This Committee was not concerned with ' classifications '. Its job was to consider the eligibility of proposed members as worthy citizens and good fellows, regardless not only of their jobs but ' of race, colour, or creed '. ' Colour ' has presented no problems to Rotarians in this country. ' Race ', too, could almost be said to present no problems here, though anti-semitism has not been entirely unknown. ' Creed ', an omnibus word, has operated to the detriment of known Communists, though the structure of the ' classification ' system reduces Communist aspirants for Rotary membership to negligible numbers; and it has not excluded anyone on religious grounds. Neither Membership Committees nor Classification Committees found themselves in the embarrassing position of having to report against candidates from ' unworthy ' or ill-regarded occupations : those pursuits, the *milieu* of 'spivs' and racketeers and exploiters of amoral cupidity, were carefully excluded from the list of the eligible.

New members were elected by the Club Council, but it was the function of the Membership Committee to select and recommend. Before the new member was enrolled and 'inducted' (a minor Club ceremony of the utmost simplicity, radically different from the elaborate 'initiation' rites practised by some of the more esoteric fraternities), his instruction in the aims and objects of Rotary was undertaken by a Committee originally called the 'Candidate Education Committee', but now known as the Information Committee. ('Education' was considered, in this context, to have unfortunate implications.)

* * * * *

Information. To meet (as a Committee) all candidates for membership; to give them full information about Rotary—its origin, growth, organization, aims, objects and achievements; to explain duties, responsibilities and obligations to Rotary as well as benefits and privileges, and, generally, to fit candidates to take their place in the Club as informed Rotarians.

This sub-committee was to consolidate the work of the two Committees already described. 'If the information imparted by the Committee is of a perfunctory nature, the new member probably enters the Club with wrong ideas and expectations, and this is fair neither to him nor to the Club'.[1] This Committee was nevertheless more likely to be perfunctory than most of the others. The candidate was usually a man whom the Club *desired* to recruit : if recruitment was following the approved procedure, he was a quarry, not a supplicant knocking at the gates. It was only too possible to frighten him off. The temptation to soften the preliminaries was therefore considerable, as was the reluctance in many Clubs to serve on a Committee whose terms of reference postulated a thorough knowledge of Rotary lore. Some Clubs accordingly 'got along' with no Information Committee at all— and some still do, despite the urgent entreaties of responsible officers at 'District' and national headquarters. A few Clubs left all the 'Information' work to some other Committee, such as 'Membership'. 'What is certainly not wise,' said R.I.B.I.

[1] 'Club Service'. R.I.B.I. Pamphlet No. 2, p. 23.

headquarters, ' is for the President and Secretary (of the Club) to interview the candidate in a casual fashion and let this serve in lieu of a proper Committee meeting.' [1] It was nevertheless what was fairly commonly done; and there are even Rotarians of recent appointment today who have no knowledge of an ' Information Committee ' or of having been ' instructed ' in Rotary by any Committee at all.

But in any well-run Rotary Club a candidate for membership met the Information Committee, at a time apart from the Club's weekly luncheon; and, perhaps after a meal, the Chairman and his fellow-members propounded to him that

a Rotarian must neither seek nor expect commercial benefit from his membership; shall not only represent his vocation in Rotary, but also represent Rotary principles to his associates in his own vocation; shall personally participate in the Club's activities; shall attend meetings regularly when not actually prevented; and shall understand that his membership automatically lapses if his attendance falls below the minimum as fixed by Constitution, unless he can satisfy the Club Council that there have been good and sufficient reasons of an exceptional and temporary nature. [2]

Fully explained, all this could be a daunting recital; and it was the intention of headquarters that a candidate should be allowed to take home the questionnaire that was to be his ' membership form ' and study it at his leisure, signing only if he then felt able to do so. The demand for a 60 per cent attendance at Club lunches deterred many honest souls. Some decided that Rotary was too expensive for them—a complaint commonly heard among Rotarians today. (As to this, the sixth of the standard By-laws for Rotary Clubs says : ' The General Council has agreed that new Clubs may not be formed where an entrance fee of £3 3s. plus an annual subscription of £3 3s. presents a serious obstacle '.) Others felt it to be as much an abuse of words to say that they would ' represent their vocation in Rotary ', since they had no mandate from their vocation to represent it anywhere, as it would be to say that they ' would also represent Rotary principles to their associates in their own vocations '—their own vocations not necessarily being interested either in Rotary or its principles. This was a mistaken view. Rotary principles were the ageless principles of justice, honesty, and compassion; these were not to

[1] ' Club Service '. R.I.B.I. Pamphlet No. 2, p. 24. [2] *Ibid.*, p. 25.

be carried abroad as some new moral specific with the name of
' Rotary ' attached to it. And the new member ' represented ' his
vocation only in the sense that the Club contained no one else
from that vocation and would be likely therefore to identify his
views as those of his professional associates.

*   *   *   *   *

Fellowship. To promote a fraternal feeling within the Club; to
foster its social life; to devote special attention to the absorption of
new members into the life of the Club; to welcome visiting Rotarians;
and to encourage in every possible way a spirit of good fellowship and
goodwill amongst the members.

Fellowship is Rotary's oldest love, its essential *raison d'être.*
Its expression in the Clubs has supplied outside critics with opportunities for derision, merriment, misrepresentation and misunderstanding; and many British Rotarians have themselves
found cause for embarrassment in the vocal acknowledgment of a
simple emotion which, to the British way of thinking, flourishes
best while it is not only spontaneous but unannounced. To
these, much of the early official prescription for Fellowship has
the quality of an attempt to define faith or flowers. ' Good
fellowship,' said Rotary International in 1916, ' is evidenced
by

1. The hearty handshake.
2. The first-name acquaintance.
3. Thoughtful attentions shown by members to each other.
4. Courtesy exhibited to presiding officers, fellow members, and guests.
5. The gentlemanly demeanour and the thoughtfulness which characterize the mature business man.
6. Chorus singing.
7. ' Stunts ' of a certain character '.[1]

The prescription never commended itself to British Rotarians.
If they shook hands heartily (and they do) it was not because of a
prescription. They used first names after a little fumbling, but
the practice has now become so widespread in British communities generally that it is no longer a Rotary characteristic.
(What remains characteristic, perhaps, is the Rotarian custom of

---

[1] ' A Talking Knowledge of Rotary '. By the 1915–16 Committee on Philosophy
and Education of which Guy Gundaker, of Philadelphia, was chairman. *Rotary
International* pamphlet.

referring at meetings to 'Chairman John' and 'President William'.) No one who goes to a Rotary luncheon can fail to conclude that the goodwill, courtesy, and attentiveness (whether or not they 'characterize the mature business man') are genuine, unforced, and unbeholden to prescription. Chorus-singing and the ambiguous 'stunts of a certain character' never took greater hold in the British Clubs than is represented by the singing of a 'Rotary Grace' before lunch and certain mock-punitive inducements to regular attendance. Speakers at the luncheons (Rotarians as well as others) have occasionally found that the prescribed 'attentiveness' fell short of immaculate courtesy, especially at the close of the meeting, when they were perhaps allowed to make their own unescorted and hesitating exit. This was undoubtedly due, where it happened at all, to the fact that Rotarians are busy men snatching a rather lengthy luncheon interval from jobs in which they are not necessarily their own masters; which also accounts for the fact that lunch-time speakers sometimes had the disconcerting experience of seeing some of their promised audience get up and leave hurriedly as the address was about to begin. These lapses were strongly deprecated by the leaders of the Movement, and it is right to say that they were rare. But it is also right to remind oneself, in this context, that attendance at the lunches is obligatory, that time is money, and that accordingly the supreme virtue in a Rotary lunch speaker is brevity.

Attempts have always been made to prevent the formation of cliques in the Clubs, in particular by the weekly re-arrangement of seating. New members have always been given special attention : one large modern Club gives them a ribbon bow to wear on their Club badges for three months, not as the stigma of the tenderfoot, but as an indication that the new member needs a special warmth of welcome to offset any strangeness. 'Fellowship', however, in its essence, arose not from the weekly *badinage* over luncheon-tables, but from the experience men got from working together in small groups on delegated Club enterprises. The luncheon meetings were too large, and the hubbub of conversation too distracting, for serious conversation on fundamentals. The abiding fellowship that flows from mutual respect and communal endeavour sprang from the work of the numerous small committees. It is in their committees that Rotarians get to know each other; and it is a general rule that every member of a Club shall be a member of one of the numerous committees.

*   *   *   *   *

Attendance. To review attendance of members; to visit or arrange for visitation of absentees; to keep in touch with members who are sick or in trouble; to encourage members who miss luncheons to send apologies to the President; to impress upon irregular attenders the importance of the attendance rule in Rotary; to report to the Council all members whose percentage of attendance is below sixty per cent; and to encourage attendance at Conferences and Inter-Club Meetings.

The compulsory attendance rule was a distinctive feature of service Clubs in all countries, but in the Rotary movement it was almost an article of religion. ' District ' bulletins and magazines regularly printed ratings of Clubs according to their attendance figures : shields, trophies, and prizes were awarded for the highest, their presentation at District and National conferences being greeted with enthusiastic applause. A Rotarian absent from his Club meeting was allowed to be counted as present if, within the six days before or after that meeting, he attended the meeting of another Club and got his ' attendance card ' marked accordingly. Various unsuccessful attempts have been made to get the ' Constitution ' altered so as to recognize Rotary meetings on ships making long voyages as ' attendances '—though this is now allowed if the members are *en route* to a Rotary Convention.

The rule was an onerous one; and the story of Rotary Clubs is full of instances in which the utmost ingenuity was employed to find loopholes in it. Any such discoveries usually led to a further tightening-up by ' legislation '. In 1930 a Rotarian who found himself at cross-purposes with the whole of his Club (an extremely rare event) announced his intention of putting in all his 60 per cent of attendances at other Clubs. Before he could put his solitary gesture into effect the Constitution of ' R.I.B.I.' was so amended as to require that a man's attendances at his own Club must not be less than 30 per cent during either of the half-yearly periods of the Club's fiscal year. The so-called ' stunts ' to which the Clubs resorted to foster good attendance were not, as a rule, necessary where the Club ' programme ' was made sufficiently attractive. Some Clubs divided themselves into two teams, each with a captain, which strove to outdo each other in attendance figures : the losing team at the end of each month paid for the lunches of the winners. Some of the less well-to-do members complained, as the novelty of this scheme wore off, that it was carrying the school 'house competition spirit' too far, and penalizing the regular attender for the waywardness of the dilatory. One of the earliest Clubs in the country, which used the 'attendance-team' method, gave the monthly winners a box of 'puritanos creme de luxe'.

It was on this question of attendances that the difference between 'Rotary' and Rotarians, between the leaders of the Movement and the mass of individuals who formed the Clubs, showed itself most markedly. Membership ceased automatically, said ' R.I.B.I.', when a man's attendances fell below the prescribed 60 per cent—'unless he be excused by the Council of the Club for good and sufficient reason'. And the permitted reasons were prescribed : meetings of a public body of which a Rotarian was a member, e.g. 'Parliament, County Council, Town Council, Magistrates' Court, Public Assistance Committee, Harbour Board and River Commissions, Juvenile Advisory Committee, Court of Referees, Pensions Committee, Jury Service, Military Service, Trade Associations '. A member could get ' leave of absence ' if he found himself unable at any time to comply with a further rule that he must not miss four consecutive meetings of his own Club; and the prescribed grounds for this were illness, accident, travel for health reasons, visits abroad, and holidays. But neither ' excuse ' nor ' leave of absence ' could credit him with the attendances he thus avoided : they merely protected him from losing his membership.

Loss of membership for non-attendance was rare; not because non-attendance was rare, but because a Rotary Club is an association offering few benefits and demanding much of its members, because it is a fellowship Club, and because it is overwhelmingly reluctant to lose men. The Club Council could get rid of a member, by a two-thirds majority vote, if he ' ceased to have the stated qualifications for membership in Rotary ' or ' failed to conduct himself or his business in accordance with the principles of Rotary '; and he automatically ceased to be a member if he (or his firm) was adjudged bankrupt. By contrast, a failure in attendance meant (in theory) that he got rid of himself. But in practice a popular or desirable member enjoyed the utmost latitude in this final respect, and there were Clubs with many members whose attendances fell far below the standard. There still are. It is perhaps an even greater domestic problem for Rotary than the fact (common to many associations) that the laws of libel and slander inhibit the arbitrary expulsion of an ill-conducted member if his conduct, however outrageous, falls short of illegality.

Programme. To arrange for the speakers for and the addresses to be given at the Club meetings; to see that the addresses delivered are widely varied in character and in general serve the purposes of Rotary; and, in particular, to see that an adequate representation of definitely Rotary subjects be given to the Club.

The work of this Committee (which in many Clubs fell to an individual known as the Programme Secretary) was obviously of prime importance to the success of the Club. In many of the larger and more influential Clubs the number of people who *wanted* invitations to speak was sometimes overwhelming. The Committee (or Secretary) concerned had to preserve a balance between speakers on the general topics on which the minds of good citizens should be informed, speakers on sociological subjects within the ambit of Rotary endeavour, and speakers from within the Movement on such matters as recent Rotary Conferences and Assemblies and the important business of running good Clubs and committees. ' Rotary ' addresses were (and are), with exceptions, the least popular. They have acquired what seems to the outside observer the holier-than-thou name of ' inspirational addresses ', and it is as rare for them to be of absorbing interest as it is for a purely evangelical church sermon to be of absorbing interest. They present to the uninstructed outer world Rotary's most vulnerable side. In October 1924, for example, a solicitor from the Liverpool Rotary Club, addressing the annual meeting of the Law Society at Manchester, told his brother lawyers that ' Rotary Clubs afforded a means of expression for the strong civic sense, philanthropic instincts, and social instincts of the legal profession '. This was entirely true and, it might have been thought, unexceptionable. But a critical lawyer rose to ask how people got into Rotary Clubs, and said that in his view the Clubs were ' chiefly composed of tradesmen who had done pretty well out of the war, and who found in the Club an excuse for a feed and for listening to a lot of drivel which appeared

F

afterwards in the local papers '.[1] This was ill-natured in a non-Rotarian (though his opening question suggested the annoyance of the excluded); but it commanded some sympathy even among Rotarians at the time, and would probably do so today. An American writer, Bruce Bliven, writing in *Forum* in December 1928, on ' The Babbitt in his Warren ', lampooned Rotary lunch speakers in a passage that is worth noting as an instance of the publicity accorded to the Movement at the time of the ' Aims and Objects Plan ' :

First, there is the product of the rank novice, the prominent business man of your own or some nearby city, who takes a long time (and it seems longer) to deliver a ten-minute speech on ' Main Developments in the Cold Storage Industry ' or ' The Trust Company : Your Friend, Your Counsellor, Your Guide '. This gentleman is usually suffering from an acute case of exhibitionism, with nothing to justify it. He dearly loves to read in public the papers written for him by his advertising man, who has been careful to work in generous references to his own company, its resources and facilities.

The other standard type, just as bad, is the ' inspirational ' address. Even today, after all the ridicule that has been rained upon this weird product, it is still being uttered, day in and day out, North, East, South, and West—especially West. Every member of every Club ought to know it by heart, but seemingly he doesn't, for he tolerates its endless reiteration.

It is no answer to my criticism to say that most of this inspirational stuff is true. What if it is ? It is also true that the world is round. But that is no reason why men should get together once a week, in a badly ventilated room, bolt down a heavy and indigestible meal, smoke more than is good for them, and hear this ancient truth expounded with fist-wavings and bellowings, for half an hour if they are lucky and an hour if they aren't.

The man who wrote that was enjoying himself too much to be master of his pen, and his joy was unholy. But his rather ill-mannered tirade illustrates more than the impact of certain aspects of Rotary on slick journalism : it shows also what Programme Committees had to consider, even without assistance from outside critics, in putting up speakers for the instruction or entertainment of their fellow members in the Clubs. The ' inspirational address ' was and is important in an organization dedicated to social service, but hardly more important than the

[1] *The Times*, 2nd October, 1924.

vehicle and manner of its delivery. Too much of it could have a serious effect on attendances.

The Programme Committee's job was not simplified by certain cautious and apparently contradictory precepts in the standard Club Constitution.

The general welfare of the community is of concern to the members of the Club [said the Constitution], and the merits of any public question involving such welfare may be fairly and intelligently studied and discussed at the meetings for the enlightenment of its members in forming their individual opinions.

At the same time, and in an age of mounting political awareness and literacy which made it difficult to isolate public welfare from political expedients, it was ordained that ' party politics and sectarian religion shall be excluded from all proceedings of the Club '. And in 1933 an agreed *Statement of Policy in Rotary Service* declared that ' the Association or the Rotary Clubs may with advantage discuss any such matters of public controversy as can be discussed *without the risk of losing good fellowship* and with care to provide for an equal presentation of all points of view '. The combined effect of these injunctions upon Rotary oratory made some members feel, as a famous critic felt when he read Ruskin, ' not that injustice, wickedness, and stupidity must be put down, but that indignation, anger, and the wrath of God's chosen were themselves palatial and satisfying edifices to dwell in '. Programme Committees picked their way through them with great care, to the satisfaction of the convivially timorous and the exasperation of the hotheads. The subsequent entry of ' politics ' into so many departments of the common way of life has given strength to the hotheads without, up to the present, damaging the fabric of ' fellowship '. But the difficulties increase.

* * * * *

Several other committees were contemplated by the ' Club Service ' division of the Aims and Objects Plan—and there was no attempt to discourage the formation of unspecified Committees to deal with local Club needs. Many Clubs had a Sports Committee, since inter-Club and (later) inter-District contests of many kinds have always been popular, the nature of the sports reflecting the fact that Rotary is not a young men's Movement (golf, cricket, bowls, snooker, and shooting). Some Clubs had a 'Public Information Committee', which arranged local publicity for such of the Club's activities as might be furthered by publicity, supervised the Club's own publications and appointed the 'Club Correspondent' who, besides sending in news of the Club's activities to the District and National magazines, in many cases edited the Club's own bulletin. But in most instances the 'Club Correspondent' did all this without a committee. A 'House Committee' was sometimes appointed to supervise menus and investigate complaints, and to look after the few Club properties— its badges, its visitors' books, its President's chair and gavel, its Rotary 'wheel' (the emblematical disc on which, in many Clubs, the members signed their names at every luncheon meeting); but in default of a House Committee these duties fell to one of the other committees or the Secretary.

*　　　*　　　*　　　*　　　*

The Secretary, however, was the pivot of the Club and its busiest man. He sometimes held office for many years (since there was little competition for his job), and this was of great advantage in an organization where the committees changed most of their personnel annually. The description of his duties in the standard Club Constitution was little more than an attempt to remember some of the things he had to do, concluding with the injunction that he 'perform such other duties as usually pertain to his office'. Some such words are to be found in all prescriptions for secretarial duty, and they necessarily leave something to the secretary's imagination. In the case of a Rotary Club they leave almost everything.

Chapter Eight

'VOCATIONAL SERVICE'

In Great Britain and Ireland the Rotary Movement puts ' vocational service ' first, as an expression of the ' good life ' which is at once the most worth-while, the most individual, and the most difficult of attainment. In America, at least until recent times, the emphasis has been rather on ' community service '—some aspects of which, however, are so ' vocational ' that Rotarians themselves have difficulty in classifying a form of ' service ' under one heading or the other (see Chapter Nine). In other countries it has been on ' fellowship '.

The only unique feature of Rotary is vocational service : everything else that we do is repeated by some other organisation. If we are unique, if we have a special message or mission in the world that is unique to ourselves, it lies only in the realm of vocational service.

That statement of Rotary's essential nature was made in 1935 by T. A. Warren, Director of Education for Wolverhampton, who was to become President of Rotary International in 1945–46. When he made it he was Chairman of the Vocational Service Committee of ' R.I.B.I.', and he was seizing the opportunity of the 1935 Conference to answer Clubs all over the country which were saying : ' We don't know what to do when we form a Vocational Service Committee '.

' Vocational service ' had been for years the one form of Rotary endeavour that appeared to lack dynamic because its results were unspectacular—and often imperceptible. To some it was a vague, pragmatical plan of living according to the Golden Rule ; to others a Wordsworthian substitute for revealed religion ; to many a means by which, it was supposed, a man could order his business or professional life on Christian lines without the awkward demands of orthodox church membership.

The middle and upper class Englishman [wrote a well-known ecclesiastic in a recent pseudonymous article] is hostile to clericalism, impatient of dogma, more interested in the moral than in the spiritual aspects of religion, disinclined to commit himself to any definitely-formulated credal position, and unwilling to submit to any binding obligations of church membership.[1]

He was generalizing, and perhaps his mood was pessimistic; but he was writing about the men from among whom Rotary Clubs are formed. The Bishop of Portsmouth, on the other hand, has told Rotarians that ' the breaking-out of associations and institutions such as Rotary, and their success, can be legiti-mately quoted as an evidence of the way the churches have gripped the mind of the English people'. These two statements are reconcilable and complementary. But if Rotary is a morality without supernaturalism, it must base itself on the Pelagian doctrine of ' the intrinsic goodness of human nature', which is essential for any progressive social philosophy.

Intrinsic goodness is the mainspring of ' vocational service'.

*   *   *   *   *

Under the 1927 ' Aims and Objects Plan', the Vocational Service Committee in every Club had its duties thus prescribed :

To devise and carry into effect plans which will guide and assist the members of the Club in discharging their responsibilities in their vocational relationships, and in improving the general standards of practice in their respective vocations.

The campaign was slow in starting. From about 1927 on-wards, as the growing bitterness of international interests was more and more clearly seen to be due to economic causes, to the paradox of ' poverty in the midst of plenty', the smaller business man tended to drift into a despairing and almost hypnotized inertia. The disruptive forces that were causing unemployment, trade strife, and class warfare seemed to be cosmic forces outside human control. The relatively smooth-running ' master-and-man' relationships of Edwardian days acquired a retrospective halo of felicity that obscured their uglier coercions. Could we not get back to the days when everyone knew his place, when many firms began the day with a short prayer-meeting attended by staff and management, when the pound was worth twenty

---

[1] ' Artifex' in the *Manchester Guardian*, 4th July, 1949.

shillings at home and five dollars abroad, when the exhortation to
' Buy British ' was a business slogan rather than a death-bed injunction, and when the only men unemployed were the sick, the
aged, and the bone-idle ?

It is in the nature of Rotary work, and especially of its ' vocational service ', that no amount of research could enable a true
account to be given of its impact on this industrial *malaise*.
Rotarians set themselves the task of ' making their jobs an opportunity to serve society '; and they saw society as comprising four
groups—their employees, their fellow-employers, their suppliers,
and their customers. The ' vocational service programme ' put
the employees first : a Rotarian who was not a good employer
would be a man belonging to a Movement which he did not
understand and in which he was an unwelcome passenger.

' Good employer ' was a phrase with a multitude of possible
interpretations, and the desire of Rotarians so to qualify themselves (in their own stimulated consciences, not necessarily in the
eyes of the Club or even of their employees—it must be distinguished from the mere quest of popularity) led to a multitude of
activities. Pension schemes, medical attendance, part-time
education for staffs, the revival of apprenticeship, advice on
careers, the extirpation of bribery and secret commissions, the
setting-up of joint industrial councils and works councils, fairness
in promotion systems, profit-sharing schemes, allocations of
profits for staff welfare and sports, the arrangement of work
schedules on humanitarian principles—all these were adopted and
pursued by Rotarians throughout the country as expressions of
' vocational service '. They had their difficulties. Cynicism—
the ' juvenile shrug-philosophy ', as Meredith called it—was
firmly entrenched in the late twenties. And ' there are many who
carp and scoff at generous qualities ', says Lord Samuel, ' in order
to justify to themselves their own lack of them.' The pension
schemes, since they must be actuarially sound and yet compete
with the ' £1000 Free Insurance ' stunts then being performed by
newspapers, were sometimes greeted as ' disguised pay-cut
rackets '. The part-time adult education classes, even though
attended in the employers' time, were either designed to get more
profits by better equipping the workers, or ' modern clap-trap '
which the foreman or overseer had always had to do without.
The new campaign against bribery and corruption was dismissed

as a mere matter of subscribing to the Bribery and Secret Commissions Prevention League while continuing to condone the
pernicious practice of giving clandestine ' sweeteners '.   Some
of the Works Councils met in an atmosphere of suspicion and were
taken up with an airing of petty individual grievances.   Many
profit-sharing proposals met with the dogged rejoinder : ' We
want a fixed wage every week, not a promise for Christmas '—and
they still do.

But the Rotarians (or some of them) persisted.   The recon-
ciliation of ' profits ' and ' service ' must be made manifest;
the manufacturer, the seller, the professional man must be shown
to be people no less entitled to an honest reward for their labour
and ingenuity than their critics among the ' workers ' and ' intellectuals '; and there must be an end to the conception of
capital-and-labour relationships as a permanent state of mitigated
civil war.   No society built on private incentive could possibly
survive if service to the community, as an outlet for ' intrinsic
goodness ', were inimical to profit-inspired business.   ' Is business too small, too sordid, too practical a thing for the dainty feet
of Rotary ? ' asked William Moffatt, of the Leeds Rotary Club,
in a 1924 article which typified an interesting reaction to the
growing heresy that ' profit ' was something to be ashamed of.

Must business men, joining an association of business men [he
went on], be told to keep off the business grass, and tie on to boys'
work or prison reform ?   And yet the modern world of commerce
and business is a sorry spectacle.   There are hundreds of problems in
the business world today crying for solution.   I earnestly believe that
this is Rotary's real field of activity and endeavour.[1]

The larger employers began to encounter the truly formidable
circumstance that the trades union leaders, with whom alone they
could negotiate the settlement of serious disputes, no longer
represented the men; no longer represented, that is to say, those
of the men who bothered about representation at all.   These
' leaders ' were carried to office on the mass vote of the apathetic,
and the apathetic could be incited by ' unofficial strike committees ' to repudiate them.   In the startled aftermath of the
General Strike, 1927 had seen the passing of a Trade Disputes

---

[1] ' What is the Real Mission of Rotary ? '   *The Rotarian*, Chicago, January, 1924,
p. 10.

Act hardly less controversial than the one that precipitated the great Conservative rout at the 1906 election. The 'sympathetic strike', in which one industry or trade supported another in a dispute that did not *directly* concern it, was made criminal; and so was a strike that was 'designed or *calculated* to coerce the Government, either directly or by inflicting hardship on the community'. Who was to 'calculate' whether the strike might coerce the Government, asked the workers? Why, the Magistrates, whether it was 'designed' to do so or not. In the political ebb-and-flow that has worn smooth the British Constitution, the 1927 Act was in its turn repealed by a Labour administration in 1945. But in its eighteen years of life it was sedulously used by some to agitate the industrial relationships it had been (optimistically) designed to stabilize; and the growing responsibility of the trades union leaders, because in the eyes of the rank-and-file it identified them with the bosses, had the same unforeseen effect. Yet an examination of the capital–labour relationship existing in the businesses of Rotarians during this period would show (with inevitable exceptions) a high proportion of successful negotiations, reflecting a policy of unusual and far-sighted patience on the part of Rotarian employers—even if it reflected, too, the smallness and compactness of their businesses.

* * * * *

'Vocational service' also took the form of a campaign to improve inter-trade relationships. Rotarians co-operated with other manufacturers and dealers, through their Trade Associations and the Chambers of Commerce, in seeking useful standardizations of products and practice, the improvement of design, 'market research', and the kind of production-planning that seeks to eliminate surpluses and supply deficiencies. It was an implication of their membership of the Movement that they refused business with suppliers whose reputation was not of the best, that in buying their supplies they forswore all forms of corrupt inducement and all unscrupulous 'cut-price' methods, and that they honoured all their contracts and reputable trade customs. But it was in their relationship with customers and clients (and those two categories were in a general sense inclusive of all the others) that they promulgated and undertook to observe what amounted to a standardized 'ethical code'. It is set out here as being generally representative of the Rotarian prescription for ' Vocational Service '.

1. Honest description of goods or services and scrupulousness in all other forms of ' salesmanship ' or inducements to purchase.
2. Development of the highest possible level of efficiency both in personal competence and every department of one's business so as to be able to give the best possible value with first-rate service.
3. Readiness to give the best possible advice to a customer or client, placing all relevant facts and information before him irrespective of whether this appears immediately advantageous or no.
4. Honesty in advertising.
5. Determination of a ' Just Price '.
6. Opposition to *caveat-emptor* (' let the buyer beware '), and the cultivation in the customer of a feeling of confidence and security.
7. Guarantee of other fair trading conditions, e.g. treatment of employees, purchasing, competing, etc.
8. Repudiation of all forms of bribery and corruption as a seller.
9. In relations with fellow-Rotarians, not to expect, and to refuse to ask for, special favours.
10. Preservation of public amenities, e.g. smoke abolition, decent shopfronts, well-built and designed factories, the abolition of unsightly advertisement hoardings, good printing.
11. Promotion of good design and quality in manufacture.[1]

It was, of course, a counsel of perfection, a Rotarian sermon-on-the-mount.   Many Rotarians fell far short of it, and there were (and are) a few who never even heard of it.   It may reasonably be doubted whether any Rotarian business man could rigorously conform to it and survive, either as a business man (since his life is to some extent a struggle for survival against competitors who know it not) or as a Rotarian (since his membership must cease on his bankruptcy).   But at the least it was an intelligible idealism, seeming to show more awareness of human perplexities than the scriptural exhortations to ' sell all thou hast and give to the poor ', or to reward stealthy malevolence in a competitor by turning to him the other cheek.   In 1926 T. G. Thomsen of Copenhagen, a man internationally known in the Movement, addressed a Rotarian conference at Margate on the ' Ethics of International Trade ', and gave his hearers the following list of unethical practices which, since it was considerably more specific, was per-

---

[1] *Vocational Service.*   R.I.B.I. Pamphlet No. 1 (1947 Edition).   Page 11.

haps more likely to convince 'practical business men' that their difficulties were understood :

Bogus 'independents'.
Espionage on competitors.
Bribery of competitors' employees.
Price-cutting and 'dumping'.
Fighting brands.
Misrepresenting Competitors' goods.
Cornering markets.
Intimidation by threats of litigation.
The use of trading stamps or coupons.
Excessive credits.
Enticement of employees.
Secret commissions.
Full line forcing.
Premiums to shop assistants.
Misleading prospectuses.
Misleading advertising and propaganda.
Copying other firms' designs or trade names.
Suppression of patents by purchase of rights.

A careful consideration of that list today may lead to a depressing conclusion as to the state of business morality twenty years after it was framed. But its importance lay in the fact that it was a list not merely of the practices considered unethical by the pundits of one trade association, one professional guild, or one chamber of commerce. It was held up to anathema by representatives of a world-wide association of responsible and decent citizens in every conceivable branch of commerce and service. Most vocational guilds, most societies founded on secular ethics have their lists of 'don'ts'. Admission to the 'freedom' of a City entails the implicit adoption of a more or less pragmatical code based on the Golden Rule. But to mix with Rotarians, at least in this country, is to find that their code goes beyond what has been called 'the psycho-social requirement for ethical justification on the part of business enterprise'. It may have served some Rotarians as a screen, but to most it was at the very least the statement of a hankering desire.

* * * * *

But what did they do ? As we have seen, they accepted the position that Rotary without 'vocational service' was not

justified as a separate organization. Their literature adjured
them to ' walk delicately and live dangerously ', though, to quote
one Rotarian's comment on this precept, ' Rotary is mainly composed of rather staid men, and staid men dislike being expected to
live dangerously or even uncomfortably—they ask for service
rather as a sedative and a phylactery than as a purgative and a
searing iron '.[1]   When, in such a context, you tell a business man
to live dangerously, you mean that he should expose his profits
to hazards both known and unknown.   ' Vocational Service is
O.K. provided you have adequate private means,' was one
Rotarian's answer to the comment just quoted.   For years this
form of ' service ' was the Cinderella of the Rotary scene.

Let it be acknowledged that for a long time ' vocational
service ' in the Clubs consisted of talk; of speeches, discussions,
surveys, planning, ' Rotary education ', of brains trusts, forums,
mock-trials (the arraignment of members before club juries on
' charges ' of vocational slackness), and group arguments.   But
members were repeatedly urged to join their trade associations, or
to form one if none existed in the locality.   ' How else ', they
were asked, ' can you carry the good from Rotary into your
vocations ? '

Moreover, in 1927 they began to act.   Members arranged
group visits to each other's works and factories.   They gave
talks on Rotary's conception of Vocational Service in schools,
boys' clubs, and technical institutes.   They formed themselves
into panels to advise and assist boys and girls in their final year at
school, and showed them round works and factories and offices.
(When the Education Act of 1944 raised the school-leaving age to
fifteen, this kind of thing was an incalculable aid to headmasters
at their wits' end to arrange syllabuses for the over-fourteens in
schools already crowded.)   They established ' careers corners ' in
local libraries, stocked with books on general and selected careers
and the choice of the most suitable.   They published handbooks,
for presentation to school-leavers, showing which jobs were
represented in the Rotary Club, and declaring that the advice of a
Rotarian on such a job was to be had for the asking.   (Some of
these hand-books had the disadvantage that the jobs were labelled
with the terminology of the American ' Outline of Classifications ',

---

[1] S. C. Church, of the Watford Rotary Club, addressing the 1936 Conference
(*Proceedings,* p. 67).

so that some adolescents may have been a little puzzled. But they were carefully and sympathetically compiled, and they showed an extraordinary understanding of the profound psychological change from, e.g., school captain or head girl to junior clerk or apprentice. They were the work of men who had had to ' make their own way ' and had not forgotten the bewilderments and humiliations of the first weeks of employment.) They served on local Juvenile Employment Committees and Juvenile Advisory Committees. Without (as a rule) intruding on their employees' use of leisure hours, they tried to take a personal interest in the younger workers, gave financial aid to local youth organizations, and facilitated young employees' attendance at ' further education ' schools. They gave their earnest attention to the elimination of ' blind-alley jobs ' in their own businesses, to the revival of apprenticeship, to social security plans in supplementation of State provisions, and to the need for discouraging adolescent ' job-drifting '. And in all this they co-operated with the National Institute of Industrial Psychology, the Ministries of Labour and Education, the T.U.C., the Home Office, the Industrial Christian Fellowship, the Y.M.C.A. and Y.W.C.A., and numerous other organizations that recognized the ' service ' value of the Clubs. The Ministry of Education in 1936, for example, asked the Rotary Clubs of Chester, Chesterfield, Hull, Leyton, Middlesbrough, Wakefield, and Wolverhampton to prepare reports on the existing contacts between education and industry; and their reports, the result of painstaking, honorary work by busy men of commerce, and quite typical of Rotary's social survey experience and technique, provide interesting evidence of the Association's usefulness to society within its own conception of ' vocational service '.

On the whole, Rotarians nevertheless kept their feet on the ground. Wild statements and purple passages are recorded in the *Proceedings* of their Conferences, products of the emotional climate of mass dedication to ideals. At the time of their utterance they evoked spirited applause. But the enthusiasm would be short-lived unless the oratory was related to the practical; and one aspect of that antithesis between ' Rotary ' and Rotarians to which reference has already been made was frequently expressed in the demand from floor to platform : ' Tell us what we can *do* '. This down-to-earth attitude on the part of the rank and file would have made it inconceivable that any Rotarian speaker should publicly declaim, as an advertising magnate did at a conference of the Advertising Association : ' I want to see advertising employed in an all-out drive for Christian morality and eternal truth. I submit that advertising is one of the four most influential and dynamic forces ever unleashed by man.   The others are religion, science, and mass production '.[1]   If a Rotarian orator embarked on a dithyramb like that, the close of his sentence would be lost in a spontaneous shuffling of feet.   Rotarians, by contrast, apply a ' four-way test ' whose frankness is as admirable as its brevity :

1. Is it the truth ?
2. Is it fair to all concerned ?
3. Will it build goodwill for the business or profession and better friendships for our people ?
4. Will it be profitable to all concerned ? [2]

Until the outbreak of the Second World War, ' vocational service ' proceeded along these lines; it was the work of individuals in their manifold callings even more than the work of committees, groups, and panels.   The course of the war, the incredible spectre of impending defeat, and the ' Dunkirk spirit ' brought out qualities in Britons that could have been called ' vocational service ' *par excellence*.   In broadcasts, posters, and circulars Mr. Churchill's Government did in fact exhort the people to serve the country's dire needs by sticking hard to their jobs; ' Go to it ' was the slogan by which every man and woman in the country was rallied in a strategic and tactical nightmare that none had ever foreseen.   Rotarians at that time, engaged as they were in a many-sided social usefulness (described in a later chapter), would not have called their intensified daily work ' vocational service ' : the term belongs to the uneasy phases between wars that are traditionally called ' peace ', the periods when economies can collapse and moral systems disintegrate through lack of an identifiable enemy, when the really effective rallying call eludes desperate leaders.   But Britain after Dunkirk was an entire country dedicated, at least for a time, to ' vocational service '.

One isolated illustration may be selected from unnumbered Rotarian enterprises of the war period to show that ' vocational

[1] *Manchester Guardian*, 31st May, 1949.
[2] *Vocational Service*.   R.I.B.I. Pamphlet No. 1 (1947 Edition).   Page 20.

service' inspired Rotarians at this time without needing the name. A Rotary 'emergency workshop' at Horsham, starting with a capital of £4, produced three million aircraft-components in two years.

But 'vocational service' *per se* needed a conscious act of resurrection when the nervous and emotional reaction of 'peace' had been in operation for twelve months. It occurred in the shape of a 'Combined Operations' scheme by which the Vocational Service Committee of 'R.I.B.I.' sought to focus the attention of all Club members on the post-war problems of industry and economics. It was a programme of study and discussion for the Clubs, to cover a whole year's meetings, and it rekindled interest in 'vocational service' to an extent that was quite remarkable. There were, it is true, Clubs that took no part in it; there were Rotarians who, long before the twelve months' survey was completed, said they were 'sick and tired of hearing about it'—and got on with their Rotary lunches. But the serious-minded members welcomed it as an answer to their oft-repeated cry, 'Tell us what we can do'; and over 100 Clubs published reports of their findings which constituted a remarkable survey of the industrial and labour conditions of the time—a vital preliminary if capital–labour problems were to be tackled on original lines. A small selection from them was published in 1949,[1] and the following examples may be quoted as typical of two opposing positions in the Rotary world of employers :

Trade Unions.

There are two elements in Trade Unionism, one favouring 'direct action' and the other co-operation. (*Blackburn.*)

The demand by Trade Unions for an increasing share in the control of industry . . . is understandable if it be remembered that the employee of today is receiving an education equal to that received exclusively in past years by his employer. (*Cannock.*)

Trade Union leaders are often self-made men (*sic*) who have risen from the bottom to the top but hang on to the customs and traditions of the bottom. (*Exeter.*)

Full application of the closed shop would end unofficial strikes. (*Hove.*)

Encourage every employee to join a Trade Union—to foster better relationship between employer and employee. (*Hendon.*)

---

[1] *Summary of Evidence : Comments and Conclusions by Rotary Clubs in Great Britain and Ireland on the First Part of the 'Combined Operations' Programme.* R.I.B.I., 1s.

No set of circumstances can be visualised where limitation of output can be justified, but the temptation is fully realised where fear of unemployment is present. (*Heanor*.)

Economic factors have forced upon the Trade Unions a policy of restriction of output in order to ration the work available among employees (but with 'full employment' this policy should be reversed). (*Derby*.)

One of the great disadvantages of the Trade Union movement is that it is a political party. Employers would be much more willing to make concessions if they knew that at the same time they were not helping a political party with which they were not in sympathy. (*Glasgow*.)

Whereas boys and men are invariably asked for their qualifications when applying for a position . . . the same method is not applied to anyone starting a business. (*Norwich*.)

As appropriate ethical standards are a condition of membership of Employers' Federations . . . the Unions should insist on a standard of proficiency and integrity in their members. (*Crewe*.)

Works Councils.

Such useful purpose as they served came to an end with the war. They serve now merely as a forum in which workers air their grievances and make criticisms of the management. (*Ramsgate*.)

With industry as at present controlled, the worker feels that by suggesting improvements he is merely augmenting the profits of the shareholders. It is a striking fact that while during the war about 50 per cent of factories had Works Councils, the percentage has now fallen to about 1 per cent. (*Glasgow*.)

Works Councils are of great value. They promote team spirit and afford joint consultation on all matters concerning the relations between management and workers. (*Liverpool*.)

In small units they are not a success, certainly not in establishments employing under 100 workers. (*London*.)

Strikes.

There is far less industrial unrest and far fewer strikes in numerically small organizations than in the larger ones. (*Croydon*.)

Strikes . . . could be largely eliminated by speeding up the machinery for arriving at settlements, but it will not be possible to eliminate strikes entirely and deprive the worker of the right to withhold his labour if he feels justified in so doing. (*Glasgow*.)

Heavy taxation makes a strike less onerous to the employer; and strike pay and refunds in P.A.Y.E. tend to soften the financial loss for the striker himself. Recent strikes have shown that the real sufferers are the general public. (*London*.)

Management.

Leaders of Trade Unions should acquire some experience and technical knowledge which will enable them to understand the problems of management. (*Cannock.*)

Bad management presents the opportunity for the workers to get control. (*Ramsgate.*)

71 per cent of factory workers in this country are employed in works which have less than 500 people on the payroll. (*Heanor.*)

We believe there are no perfect managers any more than there are perfect workmen. (*Belfast.*)

Education.

From the school-leaving age the employer comes into the picture for better or worse, and some education of the employer in methods of co-operation with the educationist is still necessary. (*Willenhall.*)

The majority of children entering a particular industry do so more by accident than design. (*Belfast.*)

When a boy has actually started work a most important factor in his approach to it, and in the moulding of his future, is the type of instructor or foreman under whom he serves. (*Chatham.*)

Many parents are not prepared to take the necessary trouble to study the inclinations and needs of their children. (*Dudley.*)

*   *   *   *   *

All the Clubs proffered general conclusions on the basis of their own findings, but none was more revealing than the following summing-up from the Rotary Club of Sheffield :

Slumps and mass unemployment are not always recognized as inflictions of a world-wide origin that harm the employer as much as the employee; but, in the bitterness of mind that accompanies a strong sense of insecurity, they are distorted to a prerogative of the employer class, by which labour is forced to sell itself as cheaply as possible and is kept in order—indeed, kept servile. Among the frailties of humanity are deeply implanted satisfaction at being able to order other people about and resentment at being ordered about. For this reason managers and foremen should be selected with the greatest of care and trained in the conscientious yet diplomatic discharge of their duties.

Two modern trends, indeed, enhance the human importance of managers almost daily. One is the growth of the ' welfare State '. The other is the sale of large private businesses, under

G

the strain of death duties and other taxation, to the investing public. But it would be to the great benefit of any country, however it might order its economy and however paternal its government, if the Rotarian conception of ' vocational service ' could inform the daily lives of its entire people.

Chapter Nine

' COMMUNITY SERVICE '

' MAN is certainly a benevolent animal,' wrote the incorrigible Sydney Smith; ' A never sees B in distress without thinking C ought to relieve him directly.'

The part of C is played, in the belief of a growing multitude of easily-satisfied citizens, by our increasingly paternal Government, any gaps being filled by what are vaguely known as the ' voluntary social services '. But it was an inevitable consequence of the zeal with which Rotarians investigated and ' surveyed ' the social conditions in their Clubs' territories, to say nothing of their vulnerability as lunch-time audiences for social welfare propagandists, that they became acutely aware of the gaps left by State and voluntary providence. Under the stimulus of the genial, Dickensian fellowship that is always fostered by performing ' good works ' hand-in-hand, they looked for the gaps and worked in them.

They did not imagine for a moment that they filled the gaps, or that their extra-club Samaritanism—which they called ' Community Service '—was more than a gesture. They knew that their constitutional avoidance of politics, of corporate articulation, and of any possible identity as a ' pressure group ' condemned them, at least in theory, to the palliation of effects rather than the removal of causes. They knew that this exposed them to criticisms of which the following is typical in its eagerness to discover hypocrisy and impugn the springs of charity :

The club members conceive of welfare work as a problem of individuals rather than a problem of society. The widow Smith is hungry : the club provides her with food. The fundamental causes of dependency growing out, at least in part, from a faulty social organization concern them little. Bill is a fine, smart lad who ought to go to college : the club pays part of the bill. The fundamental inconsistency of a society which accepts the principle of equal educational opportunity, and yet permits economic inequality to operate as a barrier to the effective expression of the democratic principle, never occurs to them. Their welfare activities, then, are all based on the acceptance of the status quo in our economic and political system. The possibility that the individual cases of distress which they help to alleviate are an outgrowth of social conditions which might be changed does not greatly challenge the service club members.[1]

They did not, that is to say, pull down the temple in order that all might share the rubble, and they did not give themselves to rhapsodical mourning that nothing else could be done. Instead, beginning tentatively with the widow Smith and the under-privileged Bill, they embarked on social welfare schemes of growing ambitiousness, adventure, and in some cases extravagance in their determination to ' get something done ' where authority forbore to venture or had failed to reach.

By comparison with Vocational Service, this kind of thing had for Rotarians a precise meaning and an immediate appeal.

Rotary has become a civic organization for civic purposes [remarked a Social Survey Committee from the University of Chicago] and what was originally a secondary and incidental function has become a major activity. To some of the older Rotarians, Community Service must suggest the tail wagging the dog, except that the dog (Vocational Service) has almost disappeared, while the tail has grown to enormous proportions.[2]

What had happened in America was repeated here. An article on ' Some Historical Highlights ' in the American *Rotarian* for February 1929 might have been written to describe the British experience :

They took up Boy Welfare, Crippled Children, and other philanthropic service. Enthusiasts came forward who urged that the whole of Rotary identify itself with one or other of these activities. . . . Platform addresses tended to drift away from Rotary's original purposes and to lay increasing stress on charitable work. Many people thought that Rotary was primarily a benevolent movement, which was composed entirely of wealthy men. Appeals rolled in for support from sources far and wide. Rotary was supposed to be able to go anywhere and do anything. At last came a moment when some of the original members saw the danger of engulfment in a philanthropic

[1] *Rotary and its Brothers.* By Charles F. Marden. Princeton University Press (1935). Page 38.
[2] *Rotary ?* University of Chicago Press (1934). Page 221.

avalanche. . . . It focused the governing mind on the problem : where shall Rotary begin and where shall it stop as a community service movement ?

The question has been officially answered (as we shall see) but the answer goes almost unheeded.

*   *   *   *   *

In this country, moreover, Community Service was developing rapidly by the time it was thus christened by the ' Aims and Objects Plan ' of 1927. Twelve years before that, members of the Liverpool Club had gone on record as holding that social, charitable, and civic work was ' outside the scope of Rotary, which professes to be a business organization '.[1] But in the First World War, as we have seen, Rotarians undertook scores of community tasks which were in no sense peculiar to their status as members of a ' business organization ', and the impetus did not slacken in the face of the great social problems to which the two wars gave rise. On the contrary, it carried the Movement even beyond the confines of its own written Constitution as laid down in an amendment, known to all Rotarians as ' Resolution 34 ', which was adopted at an International Convention at St. Louis in 1923. As amended in 1926 and 1936, this is a resolution of inordinate length which may, for our purposes, be summarized as follows :—

A Rotary Club should not engage in any general Community service activity that requires for its success the support of the entire community; Rotarians should act through their Chamber of Commerce in activities of this character. A Club should not endorse a project unless it is prepared to carry it through to completion. It should not engage in any activity that is already being well handled (the word ' well ' is highly relevant) by some other agency. And activities that enlist the individual efforts of all Rotarians are most in accord with what is called ' the genius of Rotary '.

With the gist of this Resolution in mind, it is illuminating to examine the list of local community services with which Rotarians were encouraged to identify themselves. In R.I.B.I. Pamphlet No. 3, *Community Service*, these services were divided into two groups, statutory and voluntary, though the division later proved to be too arbitrary in face of increasing legislation on such matters

[1] *The Rotary Wheel*, January, 1915, p. 25.

as education and public health, and it became necessary to combat a growing belief that 'voluntary action' was being rendered superfluous by an all-providing government. The listed services were as follows :

STATUTORY ORGANIZATIONS AND SERVICES

The Councils of Local Authorities and their numerous committees— many of which have power to co-opt non-councillors.

The Magistracy.

Employment Exchange Committees (concerning both adults and juveniles).

Courts of Referees.

Pensions Committees.

VOLUNTARY ORGANIZATIONS AND SERVICES

(a) *Youth.*

Boy Scouts, Girl Guides, Boys' and Girls' clubs, and Youth organizations generally.

Handicrafts exhibitions.

Scholarships.

Playing fields.

Pre-Service training for the Forces.

Child Guidance Clinics and Mental Welfare.

Juvenile delinquency—sponsorship of problem cases, probation hostels, approved schools, Borstal visiting and after-care.

Prevention of cruelty to children.

Nursery schools and crêches.

(b) *General Civic Services.*

Citizens' Advice Bureaux.

Free Legal Advice Centres.

Family Welfare Association.

Guild of Help.

British Legion, Toc H, and other 'Ex-service' organizations.

Rescue work.

Social surveys.

Councils of social service.

Community centres and associations.

Town and country planning.

Old people's welfare, clubs, and homes.

Housing : public utility housing societies.

Parks and allotments.

Anti-litter associations.

Abatement of smoke and noise.

Preservation of ancient buildings, of the countryside, footpaths,
etc.

Civic exhibitions.

Prison visiting and after-care.

Accident Prevention.

Special Constabulary service.

Animal welfare.

National savings campaigns.

(c) *Public Health.*

Cancer, rheumatism, and ' social hygiene ' campaigns.

Tuberculosis after-care.

Orthopædic treatment.

After-care for invalids and the disabled.

Hospital and mental home committees.

Hospital savings schemes.

Nursing associations.

Public health clinics.

Marriage guidance councils.

Maternity and child welfare.

Deaf and dumb, blind, aged, needy, cripples' and mental defec-
tives' welfare.

Wireless for the blind and bedridden.

Red Cross and St. John and other ambulance services.

(d) *Cultural and Recreational.*

Music, art, drama, handicrafts, and other cultural activities.

Cultural film societies.

Library associations and art unions.

Educational associations.

Literary, debating, and discussion societies and groups.

Historical societies.

Organizing ' holidays at home ' attractions.

The pamphlet which listed these opportunities for ' Community Service ' by Rotarians was itself evidence of the way in
which the tail had wagged the dog : when it was published, it
was a reflection of what they were actually doing, not a prescription of what they should do.   There is no item in this astonishing
list that has not engaged the active enthusiasm of Rotarians in
some part of the country.   For once, Rotarians led and ' Rotary '
followed—though, in following, it sought to rationalize and
co-ordinate the ' Community Service ' work of the Clubs.   The

pamphlet showed, moreover, an awareness of Rotarians' impulses no less acute (though perhaps less rhetorical) than the criticism quoted on pages 91–2.

The danger will always be [it said] to overstress the development of merely superficial or palliative services. . . . A community will be more prone to organize an annual outing or entertainment for slum children than the means to replace the slum, or to organize an ortho-pædic clinic than to eradicate the causes of crippledom.

Nevertheless, as we shall see, Rotary Clubs attacked the slums and their attendant evils in various parts of the country to good purpose.

But now let us reconsider 'Resolution 34'. How many of these activities can be said not to need 'the support of the entire community'? In so far as they all serve community needs, the answer is, none. How many of them could be carried to completion by the Clubs, acting (if need be) without the aid of the community? In at least half of them no question of 'completion' could ever arise—they are continuing or self-propagating demands. How many of them represent projects not being 'well' handled by some other agency? The interesting fact that would in all probability emerge from a full consideration of this question is that a high proportion of the 'agencies' now handling social needs 'well' were started by Rotarians; in some instances, moreover, Rotarians were not impressed with the work of existing agencies in social service, and they reserved to themselves the right to judge, to augment, and even (in rare cases) to supersede. . . . Finally, how many of all these activities 'enlisted the individual efforts of all Rotarians', in conformity with the injunction laid down by Resolution 34? None. They were all the concern of enthusiastic groups in the Clubs, generally even of a minority. But they afford clearer evidence than any other form of Rotary activity as to the impact of the Rotary Club Movement on the social life of this country. Since it is the special purpose of this book to record that impact, some examples of Rotary 'Community Service' will now be considered. It will be important, in doing so, to bear in mind the fact that in all Rotarian literature 'Community Service' is distinguished from the other forms of service as affording legitimate scope for 'corporate action' by the Clubs; and that here, as nowhere else,

the ' classification ' system of club membership really comes into
its own and proves its unique if unforeseen value.

*   *   *   *   *

Rotarians learned to avoid, on the whole, social enterprises
that would involve them in maintenance expenses without fore-
seeable end.   Their policy was to start only those institutions
(old people's homes, health clinics, youth clubs, housing societies,
repertory theatres, and so on) which might in a reasonably short
time become independent of Rotary, developing their own ways
of raising funds.   Some of the Clubs were to burn their fingers
badly before this became a settled principle, while others,
vicariously wise or empirically timid, resolutely confined themselves to what was semi-derisively called ' the multiplication of
occasional beneficences '.

The ' occasional beneficences ' seldom deserved the strictures
levelled at them by the disciples of planned and large-scale service.
They had, at any rate, the whole-hearted co-operation of great
organizations like the Family Welfare Association and the Councils
of Social Service, to whom the Clubs constantly applied for lists
of needy, aged, or disabled people upon whom to confer their
organized hospitality in the form of ' outings ', concerts, dinners,
and Christmas hampers.   ' Rotary have asked us to undertake a
very pleasant task for them for the last two years,' wrote the
secretary of the South St. Pancras Committee of the Family
Welfare Association in 1949; ' that is, to nominate fifty people to
have an outing to the sea.   It has given us the greatest pleasure
to do this, as their arrangements for the outing have been most
marvellously complete.   They go and return by private bus,
lunch in a private room such as many have never seen before, have
packed sandwiches for supper on the way home—and eggs for the
following morning's breakfast.'   That story could be repeated
a thousand-fold in respect of almost any year of Rotary's history
in this country—side by side with countless lesser tales of help
for individuals.   The Rotary Club of Warrington allocated £25
from its subscribed funds to help a selected few of the town's
poorer people to enjoy Christmas.   The local Council of Social
Service provided the names.   One was that of a woman with
four children, whose husband was in prison and who was herself
waiting to enter hospital for a major operation.   Her immediate

anxiety, which for the time being characteristically outweighed all the others, was that her underclothing was ' in rags ' and that she dreaded its being seen in the hospital. The Club provided her with a complete outfit; and the letter she wrote them from hospital, if it had to bear comparison with the sterner view that the episode was ' very touching, of course, but not Rotary work ', assuredly held pride of place in their minds as long as the occasion was remembered.

Such isolated, short-term kindnesses may be less open to criticism from the official viewpoint than another Club's undertaking to ' adopt ' the son of a deceased airman, an undertaking which committed the Club members (including those joining after the thing had begun) to an annual subscription of 15s. each for twenty-five years. But the ' occasional beneficence ' was always open to criticism on the ground that there existed specific agencies, organized for the purpose and much more powerful, to take care of the overlooked and the dispossessed and the socially unfortunate : Rotarians, said the pundits, could co-operate with those agencies, and they could if they wished support them with funds : but sporadic acts of charity on their own account were ill-advised.

Rotary's work with the Family Welfare Association, however, consisted mainly (as it did in the case of the Councils for Social Service, the Y.M.C.A., the Marriage Guidance Councils, and the Committees of almost every benevolent or rescue society in the country) in active representation on local committees. Indeed, in many instances the local branches of these societies were actually formed by Rotarians : they had founded over a dozen of the local Marriage Guidance Councils by 1949—notably at Leicester; and, to quote the General Secretary of the National Marriage Guidance Council :

The essence of a Marriage Guidance Council is the co-operation of doctors, lawyers, clergy, magistrates, and social workers, so that Rotary Clubs have often been in a position to promote team work without making the new venture appear to be dominated by doctors, clergy, or any other particular group.

* * * * *

Many Rotarians found a perfect opportunity for Community Service in prison visiting and in membership of Discharged

Prisoners' Aid Societies. Every prison in the country has a number of voluntary visitors, approved by the Governor and the Prison Commissioners, and they discuss with prisoners in their cells—without supervision—any topics of the day except ' controversial matters ' (which is generally understood to rule out religion) or ' matters affecting the prison administration '. At every prison, moreover, there are prison visitors who are Rotarians. (Hugh Parsons, once President of the Rotary Club of London, was also Chairman of the National Association of Prison Visitors.) A prison visitor shares in the work of preparing prisoners for their re-entry into the free life of the community; and it is a truism that imprisonment without such work, without the utmost possible effort to send a man back to full citizenship a better man than when he was sentenced, would be the most futile gesture of tribal vengeance, inevitably destined to recoil. Accordingly, the prison visitors' services are highly valued by the prison authorities. But service on the ' Case Committees ' of the Discharged Prisoners' Aid Societies is of almost equal value. These assemble weekly at every local prison, interview the men about to be discharged, advise them on their problems of rehabilitation, allocate to them (where necessary) official funds for their first immediate needs, and try to place them in employment.

The re-employment of convicted persons is a vital need of society, and perhaps the keystone of the whole penal-reformative system. Rotarian employers have always had a good record in this respect; and Probation Officers, upon whom the task of ' placing ' a probationer usually falls, no less than Discharged Prisoners' Aid Committees, who must attempt the same task in respect of men leaving gaol, will be found to speak of Rotarians with the deepest appreciation.

*   *   *   *   *

The ' service of youth ' was probably Rotary's main ' Community ' interest. The preoccupation of Rotarians with youth was perhaps a symptom of the condition that the Movement was confined to middle-aged and elderly men. In this respect, particularly, they did not always avoid ' long-term commitments '. In 1923 the president of the Weston-super-Mare Club proposed the founding of a seaside holiday home for ' under-privileged ' boys (this phase, in the Rotary vocabulary, is a favourite locution for the Victorian word 'poor'). The project was immediately popular. At that time the number of Rotary 'Districts' in Great Britain and Ireland had just been increased from eight to fifteen, and the south-western part of England became District No. 10. In 1928 a further 'splintering' made Devon and Cornwall into District No. 17. The two districts, 10 and 17, comprising about 1,000 Rotarians, shared the expense and responsibility of the 'Rotary Boys' House' from 1924 onwards; but they were joined in 1943 by District No. 6 (the West Midland Counties), and by 1949 the liability was shared by about 3,500 members, all paying an annual subscription of 3s. 6d., and organizing, through their seventy-three Clubs, a variety of social functions as a means of augmenting the funds. The house started with accommodation for eighteen boys, and in 1949 was taking thirty in addition to staff. Each of the seventy-three 'owning Clubs' could nominate boys for a fortnight's holiday and made itself responsible for the payment of 20s. a week for each boy of its choice. When vacancies were available, boys were accepted at the instance of 'non-owning' Rotary Clubs at 25s. and from elsewhere at 30s.; and the balance of cost was made up from voluntary gifts over and above the subscription rate (the Bristol Club, for example, gave one donation of £400). By 1949 more than 7,000 boys had been given a free seaside holiday by this means since 1924. A magnificent enterprise? Its financial structure is described by the enthusiasts as 'sound'—its assets, they point out, were worth £10,000 in 1949. But the scheme has critics among the constitutionally-minded. It is a 'long-term commitment'; more colloquially, 'a millstone round their necks'; it does parochially and with improvised machinery what other organizations exist specifically to do nationally and with the smoothness of experience; it involves 3,500 members of Clubs, who may or may not share its sponsors' disregard of these criticisms, in a morally obligatory levy which is occasionally to be supplemented by a special subscription no less obligatory for its façade of spontaneity. In short, it is magnificent, but it is not Rotary; and because it kindles the warmth of philanthropy and unselfishness by direct experience, instead of eliciting from some *ad hoc* society a printed receipt bearing the facsimile of a co-opted nobleman's signature, Rotarians (who strongly resemble all other men) will go on doing this kind of thing *ad infinitum*.

But their ' short-term ' commitments in the service of youth
were, by comparison, multitudinous.   True, they founded boys'
clubs by the score, but as soon as those clubs had ' found their
feet ' and earned the various grants available for them, the
Rotarians ' pulled out ' and left them—at least in appearance—to
their own devices.   In even more cases they rescued and revived
boys' clubs which were failing for lack of funds or moral support.
And many of them established summer camps for children who
would otherwise never visit sea or countryside—Bournemouth
Rotary Club's camp at Swanage being a specially remarkable
example of efficient organization and rich emotional reward.   But
few of their schemes could have had more intrinsic value, or
reflected more truly the declared purposes of the Rotary Movement, than the frequent interchanges of visits by groups of boys
between places as dissimilar as Chelsea and Whitehaven, Carlisle
and Reading.   The Rotary Clubs of these and other places ex-
changed parties from the Boys' Clubs in their respective towns for
visits of a week at a time, and filled those weeks with a minutely-
organized survey of the industrial, commercial, civic, social, and
cultural life of communities whose nature the boys could only
have dimly imagined.   A week like this, when organized by a
Rotary Club through the resources of its many-sided membership,
would have been a liberal education even for most adults, regardless either of class or opportunity; for boys from poor homes
it was an experience whose educative value was beyond all
computation.

Nor did the accredited organizations concerned with the
welfare of the young lack the support of the local Rotary Club
in any part of the country.   Rotarians took charge of units of the
Boy Scouts Association, served on their committees, helped them
financially, and provided transport for the Scouts' journeys to
camp.   In contrast to the Rotary Boys' House scheme, they sent
boys to Y.M.C.A. holiday centres and maintained them there for a
fortnight's holiday; and they gave series of ' vocational guidance '
talks at Y.M.C.A. centres to boys leaving school, away from the
institutional atmosphere of the Juvenile Employment Centres,
with such success that the scheme was adopted and sponsored by
local education authorities.   They took a lively interest in the
work of the National Society for the Prevention of Cruelty to
Children.

Our inspectors [wrote the N.S.P.C.C. Director in 1949] have received much direct aid in dealing with cases in which children of poor families needed help in regard to clothing and other necessities. Much of this help was given on the understanding that it should be regarded as anonymous. We have received much help from Rotarians when we have been seeking for the services of men to become honorary secretaries of our branches. This office includes the oversight of an Inspector's activities in a particular area, and it is by no means a sinecure.

Many Rotarians were members of the Borstal Association, the voluntary organization entrusted by the Government with the 'after-care' of young offenders released on licence from Borstal institutions—and, later, of the Central After-Care Association, which was substituted for it by the Criminal Justice Act of 1948. In some towns they established child-guidance clinics, in others they gave their services to such clinics already in being : these, as late as 1949, were still experimental in this country, modelled to some extent on the famous clinics of Scandinavia; and although they were then producing some striking successes in preventing the deterioration of mischievous children into determined criminals, they were distrusted by the sterner penologists as 'amateur' rivals of the Juvenile Courts and a denial of the purposes of the Children and Young Persons Act, 1933, which was designed to bring every delinquent child before the Magistrates. Rotarians, however, had always given much thought to the question of the criminal child, and it is a question upon which much thought often leads to unorthodoxy. No annual conference of 'R.I.B.I.' would have been characteristic without a prolonged discussion of child crime—under the current pseudonym of 'juvenile delinquency'; and under the eloquent inspiration of T. A. Warren, one-time President of Rotary International as well as of 'R.I.B.I.', whose long experience as an educationist was matched by his disarmingly common-sense approach to this baffling problem, they applied themselves to its solution with an intelligent determination that befitted men deeply concerned with the citizenship of the future. They served as Magistrates on juvenile court panels, they sponsored 'problem cases' personally, they staffed and visited probation hostels and approved schools, they gave prizes for competitions in Remand Homes, and in a few cases they opened their own homes to children from

approved schools on half-holidays. In this last respect—the
' adoption ' of approved-school inmates—they perhaps lacked
the full approval of the Home Office Children's Branch, since it
involved some risk of intensifying the unhappiness of other
children at the school, not chosen for ' adoption ' because of their
lack of appeal—and there was also the difficulty, amounting
sometimes to impossibility, of following the case up after discharge. But to some Rotarians this kind of official timidity
presented itself as a maddening inertia, inhibiting private action
on dog-in-the-manger principles. Where they thought they saw
inertia, they deafened themselves to criticism and took action.
They were not always right, but it is fair to say that they erred less
often than their critics.

*   *   *   *   *

One of Bernard Shaw's uncomfortable paradoxes in *Man and
Superman* was that ' every genuinely benevolent person loathes
almsgiving and mendicity '. Even if the Rotarians' harshest
critics were right, even if their well-known concern for children
was ' sentimental ' and sprang, as has been suggested, from a
consciousness of lost youth in the Clubs, their equally com-
passionate attitude to the aged poor was a great improvement on
Victorian ' almsgiving '. They established many homes and
rest-houses and club-rooms for old people, financing them as far
as they could, improvising and contriving where finance ran
short, giving their leisure time as stewards and treasurers and
entertainments organizers, encouraging the old people to regard
these places as an alternative to sitting alone at home or feeling
themselves to be ' in the way ' among sons and daughters with
whom they lived.   ' Look at the people on the seats in the public
parks and recreation grounds on any week-day,' said one Rotarian
in proposing the establishment of one of these ' Darby and Joan '
clubs.   ' They are there because for the time being they're in the
way at home. Their daughters or daughters-in-law want them
to get out, if only for an hour. Where can they go if it's wet or
cold ? '

*   *   *   *   *

Membership of a Rotary Club implied, from the earliest days,
the possession of those qualities of ' civic-mindedness ' that fit
men for the responsibilities of local government and the local co-

ordination of commercial affairs. Rotarians were encouraged by
their leaders to play an active and, where possible, a leading part
in civic matters, and the Club has long been the ante-room to
election as alderman, as town or borough or county councillor,
as mayor or lord mayor.   To select one Club as illustrative of this
tendency may perhaps be invidious, but the experience of Canterbury is merely typical :

The appointment of Past-President Stanley Jennings as Mayor of
the ancient City of Canterbury serves to emphasize the part which
Canterbury Rotarians take in the affairs of their City.
    The Club was chartered in 1922, and since that year only four men
who were not Rotarians have been appointed Mayor.   Other organizations have been similarly influenced, and for 21 years out of 27 a Canterbury Rotarian has been chosen as Chairman of the Chamber of Trade
for the district.
    Rotarians have also distinguished themselves in such offices as
President and Chairman of the British Legion, Governors of Schools
and Hospitals, and members of charitable societies.
    Since the Club was formed no less than ten of its members have served
as Magistrates and four still serve the City in this capacity.[1]

A Rotary Club was a more powerful influence in ' gingering '
local councils than any ratepayers' association or similar body.
If a community thought a new school was needed and the local
education authority was doubtful, it was often the Rotary Club
(or a nucleus of its membership) that resolved the municipal
doubts.   The same was true of baths, wash-houses, traffic by-
laws, bus services and public libraries.   ' Many municipal
librarians ', said the secretary of the Libraries' Association in 1949,
' are Rotarians.   Rotary Clubs in new towns, or in old towns that
lack municipal libraries, can find a suitable Community Service
objective in agitating for a library to be started.'   The story of
Rotary's contributions to municipal government and local
development, to the purposes of ' town and country planning ',
to the provision of parks, allotments, and open spaces and the
preservation of the countryside, to ' citizens' advice bureaux '
and free legal aid centres, to public health and the abatement of
nuisances—the full story would in itself be a forty-years' history
of local government.   The Rotary Movement claims no credit
for this : it is recognized that many of the men involved might

----

[1] *Rotary Service*, October, 1949, p. 16.

well have been municipal leaders if Rotary had never existed. But it cannot be doubted that their Club contacts, besides giving them strength, experience, and inspiration, were at once the source of many a valuable project which they were able to nurse into fulfilment and a training school in municipal education. Moreover, it was for a long time possible for Rotarians to throw themselves into local government elections without appearing to embarrass Rotary's professedly ' non-political ' position, because local government elections were free from their present-day mimicry of the Parliamentary political dog-fight.

In the formation of Public Utility Housing Societies for pur- poses of slum-clearance, the Rotary Clubs had the support of the Ministry of Health, of the municipal councils, and (as a result of skilful publicity campaigns) of the investing public; and some of their housing ventures were outstandingly successful, providing good and clean accommodation at low rents for people who had been living in verminous, ramshackle hovels belonging to rapacious absentee landlords. Probably the most successful was the St. Pancras House Improvement Society, Ltd., founded in 1924 through the initiative of the Rev. Basil Jellicoe, a nephew of Earl Jellicoe and curate of St. Mary's Church, Somers Town (the poorest district of St. Pancras). This young curate, freshly down from Oxford, soon discovered that parish work would be a hopeless battle while the parishioners were crowded into such squalid and degrading homes. Better placed than many clergy- men for the purpose of securing funds, he first tried ' recondition- ing ', only to discover (as all housing societies do) that a house infested with vermin cannot be reconditioned. His enthusiasm attracted an offer of a whole street of hovels at a price of £40,000. He was now a member of the Rotary Club of St. Pancras, and the vehemence of his social compassion communicated itself to the other members. They formed a housing society, raised the money in 2½ per cent share capital by means of constant public propaganda, knocked down the hovels, and built a miniature garden city at Somers Town that has served as a model slum- clearance scheme for many years. The shareholders receive a mere 3 per cent on their capital and the flats are let at 4s. 6d. per room. Turning their attention to a similar black spot at Litcham Street, in the north of the borough, they repeated the process, renaming the street after the Countess of Athlone, who opened

H

the new estate. In both instances every family from the demolished slum was rehoused in the new flats. They were then approached by Sir Josiah (later Lord) Stamp, who, as chairman of the L.M.S. Railway, was concerned in the promotion of a Parliamentary Bill for the rebuilding of Euston Station. The Government had insisted that the Bill provide for the rehousing of the residents (all railway servants) in Euston Street, which was to be demolished as part of the scheme; and he asked the St. Pancras House Improvement Society to undertake that part of the work. They did so, and yet another block of modern flats was the result. By 1949 the Society owned over 800 new houses valued at £60,000, and a considerable area of the Borough of St. Pancras was transformed.

*   *   *   *   *

In 1931 a member of the Rotary Club of West Ham called his fellow-members' attention to the existence in Paris of a scheme for supplying blind people with white walking-sticks. (It was later learned that a blind resident of Bristol had proposed the same thing in 1921, and on a small scale had actually propagated it.) The Club evolved a plan for the adoption of this idea in West Ham, and within a short time the 450 blind persons living in the borough had been supplied. One of the Club's most active members was a publicity agent, whose business took him to many parts of the country, and by constantly recommending the scheme to Rotary Clubs wherever he went he had within six months assured its adoption by twenty-eight clubs. By 1949 almost every Club in the country had followed suit, and the idea had spread to many parts of the world, including all the Dominions; some governments even made it a punishable offence for anyone other than the blind or the certified partially-blind to carry white sticks in public. The Ministry of Transport and the National Safety First Association sponsored the scheme, and it is beyond doubt that it prevented many accidents; among many episodes being an unusual one, at Newcastle-upon-Tyne, in which two blind men who had walked into a canal were thrown lifebelts before it was realized, by the presence of their white sticks on the water, that they were unable to see, and they were promptly rescued by other means.

*   *   *   *   *

It was a feature of the early nineteen-thirties, with the world of commerce and employment suffering from what was called 'the economics of plenty', that industrial timidity and a tendency to have-and-hold were immobilizing money and increasing unemployment. The Treasury itself was urging the country, by precept and by increasingly irksome example, not to spend; and the Government had foresworn any recourse to 'public works' as a means of mobilising idle workmen. The Rotary Club of Bristol revolted. It started a 'new deal' which was to be a microcosm of Roosevelt's N.R.A. Codes in America. Spend *now*, was its policy. 'Spend for Employment' became the name of a scheme that spread throughout the country, fostered by the Rotary Clubs on a rapidly increasing scale. It was condemned as unorthodox; praised as imaginative; criticized as an economic fallacy that dangerously ignored the 'immutable' rule about the effect of an increased money circulation upon commodity prices; welcomed by the Chambers of Commerce as an act of courage; hailed with gratification by the trades unions. Local mayors blessed it at specially convened town meetings, explanatory films were shown in the cinemas, every conceivable step was taken to induce business men to spend a certain sum to create employment. In London alone over £1,000,000 was released from wait-and-see caches in response to this intoxicating, disobedient, and daring doctrine. The total effect on the country's fortunes may have been far less than many Rotarians imagined, and the campaign petered out as the ominous process of rearmament began to absorb the unemployed from 1935 onwards. But the thing had been done, it had been shown that, despite the jeremiads of the orthodox economists, it *could* be done without disaster. The truth was, said its critics, that disaster was averted only because the scheme lapsed before it got too large: on any scale that really mattered, inflation and monetary collapse were otherwise its inevitable end. But its psychological effects, whose value eludes the economist in his calculations, were clearly beneficial; and the majority of Rotarians remain convinced that it was a resounding success.

* * * * *

From Bristol, too, may be drawn an example of Rotary's influence and initiative in the world of culture, entertainment, and the arts. In 1923 Bristol Rotarians and the Bristol Playgoers' Club embarked on the establishment of the Little Theatre, the Rotary Club shouldering the financial responsibility. Rupert Harvey was its first producer, and he got together a repertory company, with a small orchestra, which was capable of presenting a wide selection of worth-while plays. Its first season ran for nineteen weeks, its second for forty-seven. But ' repertory ' is a gambler's throw in this country, and by 1929 the Rotary Club found that they could no longer meet the Theatre's losses unaided. The following appeared in one of the theatre's programmes in that year :

For Bristol's prime asset, its Little Theatre, it has to thank the Rotary Club. They have given the city the Theatre. It is for the citizens to keep it going—the Rotary Club may be benefactors but they cannot afford to be philanthropists . . .

A limited company was formed to carry on the theatre, with several of the founding Rotarians on its Board. The Company ran Bristol Ideal Homes Exhibitions and other similar ventures as a means to offset the theatre's losses—one of these survives as Bristol's Annual Exhibition. But the trade depression of the early thirties proved too difficult a period for the hazards of ' repertory ', and after desultory experiments in sharing losses with travelling companies of players, the theatre closed down in 1935, the company being eventually wound up in 1940. It was, however, succeeded by the ' Rapier Players ', who formed themselves into a Friendly Society, re-opened the theatre in 1935, and despite its destruction in the Second World War were playing to ' capacity houses ' elsewhere in 1949. The contribution of Bristol's Little Theatre to the drama of the past twenty-five years, particularly as an apprenticeship for many actors and actresses now nationally famous, was made possible by the Rotary Club of Bristol.

In London the drama was represented by the London Rotary Players, an amateur theatrical company of Rotarians who from 1930 onwards gave successful public performances of famous plays at the Scala Theatre and raised large sums of money for the numerous causes which Rotarians had at heart. They were directed and produced by Stanley Leverton, a past President of the Rotary Club of London and a man with that natural love of the theatre without which no one will ever be found to endure voluntarily the anxieties and frustrations of amateur theatrical production.[1]

Throughout the country Rotary Clubs co-operated with festival committees in the organization of drama and music festivals, working in more recent years with local branches of the Arts Council of Great Britain. The Malvern Festival itself was aided considerably by Club members in District No. 6.

*   *   *   *   *

All these are merely selected examples of ' Community Service ', some of which almost merit a volume to themselves, but each of which may be taken as representative. Mention has not been made of the ' Wireless for the Bedridden ' Society, founded by Rotarians for the purpose of supplying free radio sets to lonely invalids in poor homes and ' servicing ' the sets for however long they were needed; this is now an established Society in its own right, still supported by Rotarians throughout the country, both financially and by the free maintenance of radio sets by Rotarian radio technicians   No account has been given of the Emergency Car Service in London, through which every police station had the names and telephone numbers of three Rotarians who were ready to turn out between midnight and 6 a.m. and drive people to hospitals to see relatives who had been injured in street accidents or taken suddenly ill. An account of the various Community Centres set up by Rotarians, which, with their health clinics, lectures, discussion groups, play-reading societies, and lending libraries, have meant so much to isolated communities, would occupy much further space. It may be accepted that, wherever opportunity presented itself to serve the public, Rotarians seized upon it with a zeal that might even outrun discretion. Their motto, ' Service above Self ', often provoked the sneers of the cynical. No sneers would be heard among the beneficiaries of all these schemes of well-doing, where speculation about final motives stopped short of the psychological and was gratefully happy with known human values.

[1] An account of the London Rotary Players is given in *The Romance of Rotary in London*, by Vivian Carter (1947).

Chapter Ten

'INTERNATIONAL SERVICE'

' The more I study the world, the more am I convinced of the inability of brute force to create anything durable.' This, in the reflective solitude of St. Helena, was the conclusion that belatedly forced itself upon a chastened Napoleon.

To create something durable with the weapons of peace was the concern of the Rotary Movement from the moment when it became international. But the First World War inhibited sane contacts between most of the nations, and it was not until 1921, at an Edinburgh Convention where 1,243 Clubs in all parts of the world were represented, that Rotary's present 'Fourth Object' was formally adopted—' the advancement of international understanding, goodwill and peace through a world fellowship of business and professional men united in the ideal of service'. Then British Clubs began to appoint 'Peace Representatives', whose chief function was to arouse interest in the League of Nations and co-operation between the Clubs and the League of Nations Union. Even so, the 'aims and objects plan' of 1927 did not specifically embrace this growing form of Club activity— it was not until the International Convention met at Minneapolis in 1928 that it was formally embodied in the Constitution. It has since become, for many Rotarians, the main purpose of the Movement : they take the unchallengeable position that if peace cannot be preserved, all else is futility; and they are encouraged to see peace, not as the mere avoidance of war, but as a positive and dynamic condition of human affairs to which all men must actively contribute.

*　　*　　*　　*　　*

Most Rotarians had no business links with other countries, and some of them had a knowledge of foreign 'nationals' no more profound than emerges from insular histories and the pre-occupation of the popular Press with 'comic' foreigners. Such

meetings as they had with foreigners, during brief holidays or at
Rotary Conventions, resulted frequently in the dangerous personal conviction that all foreigners were naïve, friendly, and
earnest; the efforts of grown men to express themselves in
English lent them the aspect of small children anxious to impress
and qualify for praise, and they were lovable, harmless, and mis-
judged. On this basis, international goodwill was an early
casualty when the demagogues and the sabre-rattlers got to work.
The Rotary Movement was in the forefront of the search for more
lasting grounds of understanding.

True, for some years its ' International Service ' consisted
largely in the cultivation of ' pen-friends ' in other countries—
sometimes as individuals, sometimes as clubs—with, on the whole,
disappointing results. Rotarians, and especially English ones, it
was said in extenuation, were bad correspondents and busy men.
The part of the individual, said the official handbook on ' International Service ', was to write to a selected overseas Club whose
President was in the same business or profession as himself,
' making a point of the intense desire for and the urgent need of
international understanding and goodwill '. This letter should
be written in such terms that it ' could be expanded into a more
sustained correspondence '. It could be ' vivid and personal ',
but ' controversial topics should on no account be introduced at
this stage '. (Controversy at any stage brought a good many of
these correspondence courses to an end.) If this could not be
expected of all members of the Club (and that was considered the
ideal), ' the Chairman and all members of the club's International
Service Committee should invariably play an active part '. In
case the letters went unanswered, there was a system of reporting
failures to the Secretary of Rotary International in Chicago, who
undertook to follow them up. The part played by the Club's
International Service Committee in this correspondence scheme
was to gather such information about the overseas Club and its
town as would enable a member to speak with interest, and put
up that member to propose a toast to it at a weekly luncheon.
The fact that this had been done would then form the subject of
one of the individual letters to the selected club. . . . En-
thusiasms of this kind waxed and waned. Such schemes, said
many Rotarians, were hatched by remote Committees who must
somehow justify their tenure of office; admirable in theory, they

were divorced from reality and doomed to failure; and, despite many admirable and painstaking efforts to comply and some interesting consequences, there were members who thought them futile and less rewarding than the more clamant needs of social service at home. Greater success attended a scheme under which British and Continental clubs 'adopted' each other, exchanging visits as well as news and views over periods of many years. This was especially prevalent in the south-eastern counties (Folkestone was linked with Lille for over twenty years, and St. Quentin was linked with Canterbury); and on the north-east coast, where British Clubs joined hands with Scandinavian. But a still stronger appeal was made by the more self-contained business of organizing foreign tours for parties of young people, and in some cases of Rotarians themselves, which the international structure of the Movement made increasingly possible. These arrangements were superior to the *au pair* interchanges between individual families that were prevalent in the years between the wars. Twenty or more fathers in one Club might well be expected to ensure that their sons and daughters derived the maximum enjoyment and experience from a Rotary-organized tour in foreign parts; and Clubs in many parts of Europe co-operated with that organizing efficiency for which Rotarian business men seem to possess a special aptitude.

*   *   *   *   *

It was in 'International Service' that the Movement encountered the more awkward consequences of its deliberate aloofness from public controversy. All Rotary Clubs, for example, were professedly open to suitable nominees 'regardless of race, colour, or creed', but there were English-speaking countries where race and colour could debar a man from Rotary membership as absolutely as if he were a leper. In Great Britain and Ireland, where the colour problem seldom arose in relation to membership (and assuredly formed no obstacle if it did), there were nevertheless large numbers of Indian, African, and West Indian youths attending universities, studying at the hospitals, reading for the Bar, and in many other ways equipping themselves for leadership in their countries of origin; and many of these were lonely, friendless, and ill catered-for by the faculties with whom they studied. Without any pronouncement that might openly estrange those countries where colour-segregation was the rule, British Rotarians quietly took these coloured students into their homes, invited them to Club luncheons, and sought means of improving the conditions of their stay in this country. They were not unaware that in America and the Dominions and Colonies this might be deprecated as a policy serving only to intensify the colour-problem on the students' return home. They accepted the fact regretfully and continued their policy. This is perhaps the aptest illustration of the diplomatic delicacies which Rotarians in this country encountered when, as members of a Movement now avowedly international, they began (according to their own convictions) to behave internationally.

*　　*　　*　　*　　*

From the signing of the Treaty of Locarno in 1925, when the prestige of the League of Nations was at its height, there was a gradual reassertion of nationalisms and (to many thoughtful minds) a frightening resumption of jealous sovereignties. Strained by German resurgence, French suspicion, and Italian discontent, the League began to have a ' bad Press ' : it was a trap for the liberal-minded Powers (this, in the nineteen-twenties, was the equivalent of the modern catch-phrase about ' freedom-loving peoples '); America and Germany did not belong; the great Powers who did belong could be outvoted by coalitions of States like Guatemala and Nicaragua; Great Britain would be better advised to fall back on Empire unity, economic and strategic, and extricate herself from the Geneva talking-shop. Ordinary men and women, who in the days of ' secret diplomacy ' knew little of their leaders' quarrels with foreign diplomats, now had the quarrels set out in vivid cable-language under two-inch headlines in their morning papers. Whereas it had been thought that the miraculous invention of broadcasting would ' shrink ' the world and produce a comity of closer neighbours, the proud promise that ' nation shall speak unto nation ' became less important than what the nations were now heard to be saying.

Rotarians, seeing nothing that could take the place of the League, and filled with dismay at the failure of the 1929 Disarmament Conference, gave their support (despite some internal dissidents who identified ' internationalism ' with communism and pacifism) to the League of Nations Union. ' R.I.B.I.' would not,

it is true, approve ' corporate ' support for the Union : it was
pointed out that ' collective security ' was an issue upon which
there was dissension even within the Clubs, and ' Rotary ' would
go no farther than to concede that, although theirs was not a
pacifist movement, many of the League's humanitarian objectives
were such as must commend themselves to all Rotarians as
individuals.   Nevertheless, ' R.I.B.I.' and the League of Nations
Union formed a joint central committee to assimilate such of their
activities as had a common ground and aim, and this example was
followed by the formation of joint local committees of the Clubs
and branches of the Union.

The public association of Rotary with international affairs,
however, had powerful critics in the Movement. Edwin
Robinson, who was to become President in 1935, deprecated
what he considered to be the ' cluttering up ' of Rotary with
' international economics, tariffs, free trade, reparations, war
debts, international currency, Esperanto, and international exchange of youth '.   It was not that Robinson, who spoke for
many others, yearned for an ' ivory castle ' existence that could
ignore these things in blissful aloofness.   His view was that
the Movement should not lose its distinctive quality as an association of individuals.

Don't tie the Movement down to any individual thing [he urged].
Rotary exists to encourage the individual Rotarian to apply the principle of service, not to take corporate action but to recognize the work
of existing agencies in which the individual man-power of Rotary
should take part.[1]

Within a few months a Rotarian minister of religion was telling
the 1935 Conference that Rotary might well have undertaken the
famous ' Peace Ballot ' itself—' instead of saying that Rotarians
could do as they liked in the matter '.   And he added that ' if
Rotary was going to dam the tide, it must also damn the consequences ' [2]

*   *   *   *   *

The problem of International Service was succinctly stated in
the report of a Social Science Committee of the University of
Chicago : [3]

[1] *The Rotary Wheel*, February, 1934.
[2] *Conference Proceedings*, 1935.   Speech by Rev. A. J. Costain.
[3] *Rotary?*   University of Chicago Press (1934).

An adequate Rotary programme of International service would require the thoughtful and attentive study by Rotarians of numerous complex problems which they have neither the time, the patience, nor the special training to comprehend easily, even in a period when their own businesses are being forced into bankruptcy because of the incapacity of politicians, journalists, and business men to deal realistically with these difficulties. *Here is Rotary's most difficult task of education.*

But in this country a growing number of Clubs found the time, acquired the patience, and could, to a large extent, draw upon the Movement's own membership for men with the special training. Moreover, they sought out accredited speakers on international affairs from such bodies as Chatham House, the National Peace Council, the Overseas League, the International Student Service, and the League of Nations Union; and they held exploratory discussions on such projects as 'world citizenship', the limitation of sovereignty, the removal of trade barriers, and the universal adoption of an auxiliary language. Their leaders knew that the League of Nations itself was established and sustained as the result of propaganda by voluntary bodies—the American 'League to Enforce Peace' (1915), the English 'League of Free Nations Association' (1916), and later the League of Nations Union; the work of the two former movements culminated in a pamphlet from the pen of General Smuts that became the basis of the Covenant of the League itself.

The Second World War did not shatter their hopes. In the spring of 1941 they formed a Reconstruction Committee

to consider in detail the subject of Rotary in its relation to Reconstruction, and to submit plans for discussion within the movement of the subject of reconstruction—international, economic, and social.

The Report published in 1945 on the findings of this Committee and the comparable committees in the Clubs is a remarkable document,[1] 'to which reference is made in a later chapter. It showed that 'internationalism' had been strengthened in the Movement rather than weakened by the temporary obsessions of war, and reflected a powerful reaction against the Hitler-Mussolini cult of extreme and ruthless chauvinism. The flight to Britain of so many European refugees, and their presence in business, in

[1] *Rotary Studies in Reconstruction.* R.I.B.I. 1945.

the universities, in special units of the armed forces, and in the cultural activities of the war period, were in themselves a stimulus to ' global thinking '.   Britain has a long tradition of assimilating refugees, befriending them, and profiting from their abilities at the same time; but at this period she had opportunities that were without precedent and full of promising possibilities.   Upon one of these the leaders of the London Rotary Clubs seized.

Under the chairmanship of Sydney Pascall, Ministers of Education and observers from many governments (including those engaged in the frustrating intrigues of refugee politics) were invited to a Rotary-sponsored meeting in London to work out plans for the educational future of the world.   The countries represented were Australia, Belgium, Canada, China, Cuba, Czechoslovakia, Denmark, Dominican Republic, France, Greece, Guatemala, India, Jugoslavia, Panama, Poland, South Africa, United Kingdom, United States, and U.S.S.R.   They discussed the interchange of students and teachers as residents and the establishment of a world university.   They considered what should be the international auxiliary language (deciding, with few dissentients, that it should be English).   In particular, they visualized a world organization for educational exchange, to depend for its success on non-governmental agencies combining the international outlook with deep roots in the life of local communities.   Sydney Pascall, with H. Raymond King (a London headmaster) and other enthusiasts, worked at ' blue prints ' of an organization that was to come into being on a scale they could not have dared to predict.   R. A. Butler, Minister of Education in the Coalition Government and main author of the great Education Act of 1944, ' adopted ' their committee of foreign educationists and lent the full weight of Cabinet support to its deliberations.   From that hopeful but tentative beginning grew the vast organization known today as Unesco—the United Nations Educational, Scientific and Cultural Organization.   And in constant co-operation with Unesco, Rotary Clubs throughout the country took part in the ' educational rehabilitation ' of the war-shattered countries—some of which reported ' a total absence of basic school equipment, ranging from pencils and paper to the furnishings of laboratories and libraries '.   With the advice and assistance of the Libraries Association, they made great efforts to restock the denuded and plundered libraries of Europe.   And

with motives that would have had the approval of H. A. L. Fisher,
H. G. Wells, and other world-minded historians, they attacked
the ascendancy of school text-books that were tainted with
' national ' bias.   Education, they saw clearly, had become an
instrument of national policy, brought to its lowest level of
cynical amorality in Germany, Italy, and Japan.   Indeed, the
Wells who for so long advocated the compilation of a World
Encyclopædia of Knowledge by a consortium of international
scholars and scientists would have approved their plans for a
World University, an auxiliary language, and the true assessment
of ' patriotism '.

*　　　*　　　*　　　*　　　*

While they took steps to inform themselves on international
affairs, Rotarians encouraged international study by awarding
special prizes in local schools for essays on international subjects,
and, in co-operation with Local Education Authorities, supplied
expert speakers on such matters for fifth and sixth forms.   Many
boys from both grammar and primary schools, having won a
' Rotary essay prize ', made their first contact with Rotary and its
ideas at the Club luncheons to which they were invited to receive
their prizes.

But a far more significant outcome of the marriage of ' International Service ' with the service of youth was the initiation in
1946–47, as a permanent memorial to Paul Harris, of the ' Rotary
Foundation Fellowships for Advanced Study '.   This scheme,
in which ' R.I.B.I.' now participates but of which it was not the
instigator, developed from the idea of a Rotary Endowment to
' perform some great educational service to mankind ', which was
first adumbrated at an international Rotary Convention at Atlanta
in 1917.   Beginning with a few hundred dollars, the Endowment
by 1948 had accumulated funds of £500,000, and it now awards
upwards of fifty fellowships a year to ' exceptionally qualified
young men and women ' from the Universities of the world,
enabling them to have a twelve months' post-graduate course
(in any approved field of study) at a university in some country
foreign to them—provided that country contains Rotary clubs.
Its avowed purpose is to ' enlarge the opportunities of the
potential leaders of tomorrow to serve humanity '.   The award
of a Fellowship covers all travelling expenses from the student's

home to the university selected (as well as to the other places he visits), all tuition fees, living accommodation for the year of study, and fares home at the end of the year. Any Club can nominate a student for a Fellowship, the procedure being the concern of the International Service Committee. During his year, a Fellow is expected to travel and make as many contacts as he can without hindering his academic studies. He addresses Rotary Clubs in the country he is visiting, interpreting to them in his own way the customs, traditions, wishes, and beliefs of his own people; and for six months after his return he addresses Clubs at home on his experiences and impressions. For these reasons he is chosen for the award with the greatest care—the list of qualifications drawn up for the guidance of selection committees is a list of resounding moral superlatives that most men would find humbling to read. The possibility of a mistaken choice seems remote. Two consequences flow from this : first, Rotarians see these youthful ambassadors (they must be between twenty and twenty-eight years of age but may be of either sex) as people uniquely qualified to supplement, in ordinary human terms, the guarded and often platitudinous statements of professional diplomats and the wilder comments of the less responsible newspapers. In return for a year's training and travel, the selected student talks to Rotary Clubs informally, frankly, and with complete freedom from ulterior motive. Secondly, as the universities become acquainted with the standard of probity and excellence required by Rotary of its nominees for the Fellowship, they welcome the students selected with increasing enthusiasm. Among the numerous post-graduate scholarships known to the universities of the world, Rotary Foundation Fellowships already stand high.

*   *   *   *   *

These and other similar measures are making Rotary an international Movement. For years it was a world Movement, but that is not the same thing : the integration that holds together the Red Cross Organization, the Salvation Army, the Y.M.C.A., the Boy Scouts' Movement, was lacking from the Rotary Movement until Rotarians gave their enthusiasm to 'International Service'. This aspect of their work, which had no place in their original plans, is growing and becoming vocal. In 1933 it was possible for a national Conference to pass unanimously a resolu-

tion 'urging H.M. Government to support an International
Convention for the Prevention of Bribery', and in the next
breath to withhold its support for a resolution condemning the
private manufacture of armaments for China and Japan. Ten
years later the appetite for 'corporate resolutions', though still
strong, was under control; and Rotarians had found a stronger
taste for personal action through the established, non-Rotarian
agencies. They now supply 'consultants', at the request of the
United Nations Organization, to the U.N.O. Constituent Assemblies, and 'observers' at sessions of the Security Council, the
Economic and Social Council and its subsidiary organs (in particular the World Health Organization, the Food and Agriculture
Organization, and Unesco). They support week-end lecture
courses on international affairs promoted by the Workers' Educational Association, the University Extension Committees, the
United Nations Association, and the Council for Education in
World Citizenship. They co-operate with the Youth Hostels
Association, now a vast organization of international scope, in
the exchange of youth with other countries—and there is nothing
that they do with greater enthusiasm than this, or with happier
results.

It may well be that, seen against the daunting background of
world affairs, all that they do amounts to little more than a
gesture; and it is quite certain that it is of less significance than
many Rotarians would wish to believe. Its effect, however,
cannot be calculated, nor could a calculation be expressed in com-
municable terms. It is far better done than not done. In the
state of the world today, it is more realistic than the wringing of
hands. And it serves to canalize a valuable impetus towards
the realization by the rulers of mankind that war between the
nations has become as great an anachronism as war between Kent
and Surrey.

Chapter Eleven

WAR TASKS

THE experiences of the Clubs during the Second World War, which might have been expected to weaken the Movement irremediably, proved to be a source of increasing strength. In the years that saw the rise of the European dictatorships, Rotarians had watched with growing distress the disbandment of Clubs in the totalitarian countries, beginning with Germany; and the formula in which the dissolutions were announced had become depressingly familiar : " Italy has developed a new political philosophy which has overcome individual thought as the structural defect of a whole epoch, and has replaced it by community-conscious thought." The National Council of Italian Rotary, in fact,

considering that the objects of the Association in Italy find their best expression and most efficient realisation in the programme and policy of the régime and in the tenacious and far-seeing work of the Duce for the achievement of a just peace among all peoples . . . resolves that the Rotary Clubs of the District (i.e. District No. 46—Italy) be dissolved on December 31st, 1938.[1]

Deceiving no one, this formula intensified in the minds of many Rotarians the belief that individual thought, so far from being the ' structural defect of a whole epoch ', was the hope of the entire future of man. Exaggeration of the importance of institutions could, they perceived, lead to world catastrophe, as with National Socialism. Jews, Marxists, Freemasons, Catholics, Rotarians, the German Parties, and finally the French, British, and American peoples became arch-enemies for Hitler—in that order. As a voluntary society of individualists, the Rotary Movement in this country gained in stature with the advent of war, and the Clubs emerged as stronger and more self-sufficient units than ever. ' At this time ', wrote the President of the Association in October 1939, ' when every Briton is putting forth his most resolute

[1] *The Rotary Wheel*, December 1938.

endeavours to help the country and its allies to win through in this great trial of endurance—

I would . . . counsel each Club to do that *which it individually considers best* in lending its co-operation in local efforts to help the nation. Each Club must think out the matter for itself, so that there may be no cramping of initiative or hampering delays caused by any inclination to wait for direction from Headquarters. In this temporary decentralization of effort to save time, I would wish that each Club exert its fullest freedom to play its part in whatever comes first to mind in its own area.

Many Clubs welcomed this as a wise step, which acknowledged that the Club was the vital unit in the organization. Others saw it as a complete and undignified abdication of leadership. Perhaps both were right, wisdom not being necessarily synonymous with dignity. At all events, the Clubs throughout the country decided, as a first step, to continue with their weekly meetings, despite misgivings engendered by the Government's policy of discouraging concentrations of people in places vulnerable to air attack. There is ample evidence in contemporary Rotary literature that the meetings were a stabilizing influence, whose value increased as the war progressed from the preparatory stalemate of the first twelve months to the *crescendo* of violence it later became. There was work for Rotarians to do, there was the sweetness of community in doing it, and there was the fact that the weekly meeting was at all times the essential root of the Movement, the means by which its manifold acts of social service were related and sustained.

* * * * *

There were 497 Clubs at the outbreak of war, and although by January 1940 this number had been reduced to 486 by the 'evacuation' of business and similar causes, both the totals in membership and the percentage of attendances had actually increased. True, some Clubs had stopped admitting new members, but this was strongly deprecated by the General Council, who pointed out that the only possible basis for a successful Club was the continual acquisition of new members (of the right kind). When enemy bombing began in earnest, a serious falling-off in Club attendances might have been expected, but instead the members chose to accept the danger as a challenge to their determination to get together at least once a week. Indeed,

I

what some Rotarians themselves have always regarded as the
'fetish' of high attendance figures was pursued at this time with
an enthusiasm that might well have been foolhardy and a considerable disservice to the public interests. A Rotary Club
meeting is, in many cases, an assembly of a local community's
leading citizens and municipal officers. During the war, owing
to the purely municipal structure of the Civil Defence service,
based as a rule on the Town Clerk as 'A.R.P. Controller', a
Rotary Club meeting brought under one roof many of the key
personalities concerned in the defence of the town; and a 'direct
hit' during a bombing raid, which could have killed fifty or a
hundred such men together, would have thrown a heavy burden
on the services of surrounding boroughs. There were many
casualties among Club members, and many meetings were hastily
adjourned at the bidding of air-raid sirens or gun-fire; but there
was no instance in which a Club was actually bombed during a
meeting. The Rotary Club of Plymouth, having seen several of
its chosen cafés destroyed in succession, found itself in June, 1941,
in a devastated city with no remaining premises where it could
meet; and it moved its few surviving belongings into the sports
pavilion of Plymouth College, and held its meetings there. In
London, the West Norwood Club was 'bombed out' of eight
places in less than two years (and moved stoically into a ninth),
but prided itself not only on the fact that it 'never missed a
meeting' but on having 'led the District attendance records for
many of the war months'. In the heavily-bombed areas these
experiences were typical, yet very few Clubs ceased to function.
Moreover, at the end of the war's first twelve months the total
membership of the Movement had fallen by only 2 per cent, and
the reduction was temporary.

* * * * *

Another challenge of a quite different nature was met with
varying degrees of determination and success. In terms of what
they called 'Vocational Service', the Clubs found that the
war atmosphere created economic and psychological difficulties
for business men that could be regarded as an inspiration in themselves. They could resolve to combat the angry opportunism
which, on so many lips, found expression in the phrase 'I suppose
you know there's a war on?' The opportunities confronting

them were illustrated in a letter written in 1941 by a non-Rotarian business man in London, a representative of the distributive trades, to the headquarters of the Movement.   He was concerned with the ' distributing industry ' of the country, whose power to help or hinder, cheer or depress the purchasing public he recognized as immense.

I have studied this great public service of ours for many years [he wrote], and I fear that the war is getting the better of us.   We are in danger of forgetting courtesies, and above all we are apt too easily to neglect all the things that once we did because it ' paid '.   A message to the shopkeepers of England as a body, or a message to all your Clubs, would be a great effort towards safeguarding all those things for which we fight.[1]

The message to the Clubs duly followed, exhorting the members to ventilate and criticize in their Chambers of Commerce and their Trade Associations the new situation in which ' the customer was always wrong '.

In their desire to help forward the great campaign of war-time production, Rotarians throughout the country addressed their minds to the formation of ' productive groups ' of small enterprises for handling Government contracts.   It was a feature of these schemes that the contract firm should not always retain the particular manufacture which was the most profitable, but should spread it evenly among sub-contractors, at fair prices. Arrangements were made for the interchange of machine tools. Rotarians were enjoined to eschew such practices as the payment of excessive wages merely in order to reduce Excess Profits Tax liability, the refusal of contracts on the ground that ' E.P.T.' might claim all the profits, or on the ground that the equipment or expansion would not be required for peace-time production, the employment of unskilled or unsuitable men whose object was to avoid National Service, the purchase of supplies in the black market, the favouring of picked customers at the expense of others with goods in short supply, and veiled ' conditional selling '.

Nor were they blinded, by the frightening needs of the moment, to the great social and industrial problems that must follow even a ' victorious ' conclusion to the war.   It was in November, 1940, that Mr. Ernest Bevin, then Minister of Labour

[1] *Rotary Service*, September 1941, p. 12.

and National Service, chose the Rotary Club of London as his platform for the Cabinet's first announcement of the 'Beveridge Plan' for social security by compulsory insurance. And at that time, when many thoughtful men were trying, in desperate secrecy, to accustom their minds to the grim prospect of a negotiated peace, or even of a Nazi victory, equally thoughtful men in the Rotary Movement were doggedly working out plans for the reconstruction of a world economy in which the defeated Axis Powers would for years be crippled passengers. By November, 1941, Reconstruction Committees had been formed in 287 of the Clubs; the General Council had published a *questionnaire* in pamphlet form, designed to concentrate attention on the economic and social problems to be solved, and over 15,000 copies were bought by members of the Clubs; reports of their consequent deliberations and proposals—the proposals, it should be remembered, of experienced business men concerned as never before to make business take on some of the characteristics of a social obligation—were welcomed and considered by the then Ministry of Reconstruction.

*   *   *   *   *

'Community Service' activities during the war were multitudinous, as might have been expected. Three months from the outbreak of war, Clubs in all parts of the country were engaged in the provision of Citizens' Advice Bureaux (in collaboration with the National Council of Social Service), of clubs for 'evacuees' of all ages, of blood-transfusion centres, of 'first-aid' classes and trailer ambulances, of allotment societies, of shoe-repairing services for evacuated children, of hostels, canteens, and other recreational facilities for troops and war workers, of libraries, radio, furniture, games, and warm clothing for troops in lonely units, of personal service in Y.M.C.A. Clubs. They provided warm clothing for poor children in the 'reception' areas, wrote letters home for them, met their parents in cars when they came on visits, and arranged entertainments and sports for them. They gave their services on committees to co-ordinate war-time charitable and social welfare services for both military and civilian needs. . . . One story may be selected as typical of the way in which many of these enterprises began.

The Chairman of a District, present on one of his official visits

at a Club luncheon meeting, was asked if he would address
the Club, as the announced speaker had failed to appear.   No,
he said; he would prefer to see how they got themselves out of
their predicament.   The Club president thereupon asked whether
any member had any ' grouses '; and a member stood up to say
that there were always present in the town a number of troops and
nurses for whom no hostel or place of rest and relaxation was
provided, that other towns had already coped with such needs,
and that the Rotary Club should do something about it.   In the
discussion that followed, a landowner member offered the use,
rent free, of a large house about to fall vacant.   The vicar of
the parish, who was the custodian (on behalf of the Red Cross)
of a store of chairs and tables, then announced that this was
one of the purposes for which he was authorized to use them.
And in less than three months the Club had established a busy and
successful hostel.   The amount of voluntary labour, organization, and improvisation that went to make this possible will need
no description : it typified thousands of similar undertakings on
the part of voluntary bodies of many kinds.   But the whole
episode also typified the means by which many Rotarian acts of
war-time ' community service ' were conceived and brought to
fulfilment.

By January, 1941, the Clubs had equipped and supplied to the
War Office eight military ambulances specially built for service
with the fighting forces, and three mobile X-ray units, at a total
cost of nearly £10,000.   Thereafter, as donations for this purpose
continued to come in throughout the war, they were given to the
British Volunteer Ambulance Corps for similar purposes.   But
sums of money of this order were sometimes raised for war
purposes by a single Club : the Liverpool Club, for example,
had by December 1940 raised nearly £9,000, by the sale of old
gold and silver plate, on behalf of a fund for the ' welfare of
men and women of Merseyside ' administered by the Lord Mayor
of Liverpool.   Before the Government's colossal War Damage
Compensation scheme had been devised and brought into operation, some Rotary Clubs established Air-Raid Distress Funds that
handled and distributed many thousands of pounds for the rehousing of ' bombed-out ' people; in many cases they supplied
and furnished rest houses for people who had lost their homes.
In 1944 there was opened in Birmingham a ' probation hostel ' for

delinquent children whom the magistrates had sought to save from prison : the hostel was initiated, and financed to the extent of £3,000, by members of the Rotary Club, five of whom still serve on the hostel's committee of fifteen.

But, in addition to spending their money on such a generous scale, some Rotarians in every town gave their enthusiastic support (as might have been expected) to Lord Kindersley's campaigns for the encouragement of ' War Savings ', speaking at special meetings, organizing ' war weapons weeks ', and devising schemes in their own businesses for the encouragement of thrift. On this question there were, inevitably, sceptical murmurings in the Movement among those men who recognized the War Savings Campaign as a disingenuous means of warding off inflation, a means that could be justified only by the urgency of its end. There was nothing patriotic, they said, in lending to the Government, for a safe $2\frac{1}{2}$ per cent, money for which every other conceivable use had been stopped; nor did you thus increase the country's armament by a single aircraft, tank, or gun. But even if you thought you did, why seek to make $2\frac{1}{2}$ per cent out of it, and at the same time denounce (as Rotary Clubs had previously gone on record as doing) the private manufacture of armaments ? If any man felt that the Government should hold his money lest he be tempted to spend it on non-essentials, let him lend it to the Government free of interest. And there were, indeed, many Rotarians who did precisely that. There were even some who gave considerable sums outright, although these (said their critics) could have achieved the same effect by burning the bank-notes.

Generally speaking, the members of the Clubs kept their feet on the ground in relation to the financial aspects of the war. There was a good reception for a pamphlet on ' Monetary Systems and Theories ' written for ' R.I.B.I.' by Professor G. D. H. Cole; it was widely discussed in the Clubs (where, of course, it was also criticized as being ' political ', a charge which Professor Cole was at some pains to refute in a letter to the editor of *Rotary Service* [1]); and it may have administered the *coup de grâce* to any lingering effects of a mild flirtation with the apostles of Social Credit.[2] Rotary publications carried many war-time articles on subjects such as the National Debt, the meaning of money, the system of international tariffs, the use and abuse of

---

[1] August, 1943. Page 24.　　[2] See the *Rotary Wheel* and *Service* for 1933 *et seq.*

private enterprise, reparations, and the importance of some kind of successor to the Bank for International Settlements; and the correspondence which these provoked showed that members of the Clubs were fully aware that coming problems would call for solutions previously branded as heresies. In June, 1944, the Clubs of greater London published a series of recommendations for 'post-war reconstruction' that might credibly have issued from Transport House. It advocated a world rationalization of production according to geographical aptitude and universal need; the limitation of profits and of speculation; the nationalisation of the banks, of credit, and of transport; the control of industry 'so as to afford an adequate standard of life for all'; the wresting of currency control from financiers and vested interests—'even retail traders, if they fail voluntarily to co-operate and concentrate their individual business, to come under a governmental organization set up with compulsory powers'; the drastic overhaul of land tenure on the principle that 'all land is fundamentally the property of the State'; the elimination of the middleman; the direction of labour and the planned location of industry; a State medical service; and a vast new plan for education.[1] A symposium of the views expressed by Clubs throughout the country was published by 'R.I.B.I.' in 1945, and contained the following expression of opinion from the same group of Clubs:

Repetition of the experience of 1919–1924 and onwards, when certain vested financial interests fought reform and reconstruction on the plea that 'the country cannot afford them', must certainly be avoided this time. Lord Keynes has expressed his considered view that anything that is physically possible is financially possible. Despite the authority of Lord Keynes, who is economic adviser to the government and a Director of the Bank of England, and whose views, expressed after the last war in his book *The Economic Consequences of the Peace*, have been justified by subsequent events, financial interests will in all probability endeavour to obstruct the path of reform and reconstruction on the grounds of excessive cost. If they succeed, Barlow, Scott, Uthwatt and Beveridge will have wasted their time and the country's money.[2]

They did not succeed. But those words were written in the emotional climate of war, when the incidence of war was still

---

[1] *The Romance of Rotary in London*. Vivian Carter, 1947. Pages 235–6.
[2] *Rotary Studies in Reconstruction*. Page 164.

being uneasily attributed to economic nationalism and the reckless
pursuit of private profit. Six months after they were published,
a Socialist Government with a huge majority had embarked on a
legislative campaign which was to give effect to nearly all of them.
But the emotional climate had changed. In the reckless
spirituality of war, a man could return from an air-raid shelter
in the morning to find his home destroyed, shrug, and go off to
work. On what Mr. Churchill had been calling the ' sunlit
uplands ' of peace, the sense of property reasserted itself. Only a
war, perhaps, could wring from Rotarians a ' corporate declaration ' on a political question. Only a war that threatened total
destruction could make that declaration so emphatically and
irretrievably radical in character. Only the aftermath of such a
war could so bitterly vindicate the peace-time Rotary policy of
avoiding polemical declarations of all kinds.

*   *   *   *   *

The problem of ' International Service ', still the most difficult
in the Rotary programme of ' aims and objects ', was clouded by
the war, which might have been despairingly accepted as the collapse of all that this branch of Rotary work stood for. Instead,
the Clubs were exhorted to develop their ' correspondence
scheme ', writing regularly to overseas clubs and members ' to
ensure the preservation of the International Service framework
against the time when the bitterness inseparable from a state of
war shall have abated, in order to expedite a return to international good feeling when circumstances permit, and to help to
bring about a peace settlement free from the war spirit and the
spirit of revenge '. And they were to set up study-groups to
consider ' The Future of World Government '.

All this they did, to what effect it would be impossible to say—
apart from a quite obvious psychological effect on the men
themselves. But in addition, and until the full blast of war struck
this country in its turn, they raised funds for the relief of war-
stricken countries in Europe, the Leicester Club leading the way
with a gift of £250 to Finland in January, 1940. They organized
welfare and hospitality work among the growing number of
European refugees, the District Councils appointing Rotarians
to form links with the Refugee Councils established by the
Government in each of the twelve Civil Defence Areas. They

entertained Dominion and Allied troops in this country at their luncheons, and ' took them in hand ' for a day's companionship at a time. They ' adopted ' prisoners of war in enemy hands and sent them supplies and letters—this was done on a large and successful scale, resulting in an accumulation of names and addresses that often enabled anxious relatives to trace their missing men. In London, at the suggestion of a refugee Rotarian from Poland, the Clubs established an ' Inter-Allied Rotary Outpost ', a cosmopolitan, fortnightly luncheon-club for Rotarians of all nationalities being in or passing through London.

The Rotary Movement in this country was thus proclaiming with the silent eloquence of action what it thought about the war. But the Movement was allegedly ' international '. Its suppression in the enemy countries was known to have been dictated and purely physical. At the outbreak of war, the General Council of ' R.I.B.I.' had declared its view that ' it is now clear beyond doubt that Great Britain and France are fighting in this war for the preservation of precisely those principles to which Rotary is dedicated '.

If this was the view of American Rotarians, too, the fact was not reflected in the official pronouncements of the ' International ', which had declared in 1928 that ' it is the first duty of a Rotarian to be at all times a loyal and patriotic citizen of his country ', and which, soon after the outbreak of the war in Europe, announced that ' Rotary Clubs should not become involved in national or international politics, and should not become propagandists for or against any cause of national or international concern.'

This was taken (by many British Rotarians) to mean that the war was not a ' Rotary war ' and that Rotary Clubs should keep out of it. It might have been expected that when Rotary ' internationalism ' was put to so embarrassing a test, this would be the result; a renewed, if uneasy, invocation of its tradition of withdrawn and silent contemplation. But, in this country at least, there appears to have been an articulate body of opinion which did not expect it, and which said ' he who is not for us is against us '. American national policy, said a leading article in *The Rotary Wheel* for November, 1939, like the American political structure, was the one national brand which, under the title of ' international ', Rotary was expected (by America) to adopt.

There grew up a formidable body of opinion that the policy of ' Chicago ', by supporting the non-participation of the United States in the war (even though that fell short of complete neutrality) was ' a betrayal of all that Rotary stood for '. In *The Rotary Wheel* and its quarterly companion, *Service in Life and Work*, editorial attacks on American non-belligerency and the ' International's ' support of it reached a *crescendo* of bitter raillery which, in the estimation of a majority of the Movement's officers, boded ill for the future of the Movement—as an ' International '. These attacks had their counterpart in many responsible newspapers, and the Government itself was sponsoring broadcasts to America by British publicists with a known American following, to say nothing of American lecture tours by British politicians, all designed to ' bring the U.S.A. into the shooting war '. But they were deplored by many Rotarians in this country who, besides having friendly contacts in America, were able to visualize the position in reverse, with America perhaps fighting a Pacific war ' for freedom ', Britain watching neutrally, and ' R.I.B.I.' under fire from Chicago for not beating the war-drum. It was, moreover, significant that the criticisms were not levelled at Sweden, Switzerland, Eire, and the other neutral countries wherein Rotary Clubs were similarly dedicated to the international ideal and the championship of liberty : the call was made to America, not to Rotary, to the big battalions, not to the philosophy of world-fellowship.

Resentment of these criticisms mounted, both in Great Britain and in the U.S.A.; although there were still Rotarians in both countries who were enjoying this departure from the ' timidity and circumspection ' that had always sapped the virtue of official Rotary utterances. America's involuntary involvement in the war by the Japanese air attack on Pearl Harbour on 7th December, 1941, barely preceded an abrupt change in the editorship of British Rotarian journalism (which might nevertheless have felt, in relinquishing office, that its campaign had succeeded). *The Rotary Wheel* and *Service in Life and Work* (the latter had ceased publication at the end of 1939) were combined in January, 1941. In 1942, after the February issue a new editorship ushered in a régime of innocuousness which, for a time, had by comparison a singular lack of vivacity. It was the close of a stormy chapter. A year later, with the U.S.A. now deeply involved in the European

war theatre and American troops beginning to arrive in this
country in force, Rotary was represented on the Council of the
'Associates for Anglo-American Understanding', which in
August, 1943, joined forces with the English-Speaking Union to
form the Institute for British-American Understanding. British
Rotarians were encouraged to support the Institute by personal
'affiliation', by contributing to its funds, by entertaining in the
clubs its accredited speakers on 'Anglo-American subjects', and
by using its resources of information for the maintenance of
Rotary discussion groups. Like other international movements
whose structure had been severely strained in the earlier part
of the war, Rotary found its perplexities and embarrassments
resolved by the march of events; and Rotarians felt themselves to
be once more united under the following formula, promulgated
(almost as though speech had suddenly become possible in a
nightmare) by the 'International' at its Toronto Convention
shortly after the attack on Pearl Harbour :

The full attainment of the Rotary ideal of service can only be
achieved in countries where there is liberty of the individual, in freedom
of thought, speech, and assembly, freedom of worship, freedom from
persecution and aggression, and freedom from want and fear. *Where
this liberty does not exist Rotary cannot live.*

That statement is known to Rotarians as 'Rotary in a World at
War'. But among them there is now to be heard the opinion
that, in relation to the frightening decline in the status of the
individual and the growing disregard by modern States of the
dignity of human personality, it applies without modification to
Rotary in a world at peace.

Chapter Twelve

KINDRED MOVEMENTS

I. THE 'INNER WHEEL'

FROM the time when the idea of Rotary Clubs became a 'Movement' with wide social purposes, as distinct from a mere formula for an exclusive luncheon club, it was inevitable that women would sooner or later participate. The question was whether they would do so as Women's Rotary Clubs, with an exclusively professional and business membership, or as Clubs (which would not be Rotary Clubs) composed of Rotarians' wives and daughters.

On 1st November, 1923, a proposal that the views of Rotary Clubs throughout the world be obtained on the question of forming Women's Rotary Clubs was submitted to 'R.I.B.I.' in the form of a letter signed by Lady Rhondda, editor of *Time and Tide*, Lady Astor, M.P., Lady Parsons, Dr. Winifred Cullis, Miss Maud Royden, Mrs. Wintringham, M.P., Mrs. Le Mesurier, Mrs. Archdale, and Mrs. H. F. Wood, sister of Lord Hailsham (then Lord Chancellor). At the R.I.B.I. Conference in 1924 the proposal was explained to the assembled Rotarians by Mrs. Wood, and a long and cautious discussion ensued. The spoken objections were that 'ninety per cent of the women who had been helpful to the Movement' would not be eligible for admission to Rotary Clubs —they had helped because they were the wives and daughters of Rotarians; and that the 'International' had already turned down such a proposal, at a Convention at Duluth in 1912. The unspoken objection was that many men wanted to keep the Movement (at least under its established name) to themselves. But the 1924 Conference decided by a large majority that the ladies' proposal should be recommended to Rotary International for consideration at its next Convention. And in due course that Convention (international but always overwhelmingly American) rejected it emphatically.

But in October, 1922, by which time there were ninety-five Rotary Clubs in Great Britain and Ireland, the wives of Manchester

Rotarians had held a meeting to discuss a proposal for *organized* co-operation (as distinct from individual, wifely help) with the city's Rotary Club in its social service activities. After three months' preparatory work, during which the women's acquaintanceship ripened into the community-consciousness needed for the foundation of a Club, it was formally established in February, 1923. Mrs. Oliver Golding, the pioneer in this new venture in women's social service, suggested that it be called the 'Inner Wheel' Club of Manchester, a modest derivative of 'Rotary's' adopted symbolism that might be expected to propitiate the men. (A similar Club had been formed in Liverpool in 1923, though it did not adopt the name 'Inner Wheel' until 1926.) Club rules were formulated which served as a model for all subsequent 'Inner Wheel' Clubs until they were 'associated' in 1934; but many of those Clubs, formed by Rotarians' wives in various towns with no knowledge (as a rule) that more than one town was thus active, adopted other names. In Bristol the women's Club, formed in 1924, called itself even more modestly 'The Auxiliary to the Rotary Club'; in Norwich and Canterbury the women's Clubs, established also in 1924, were respectively the 'Ladies' Auxiliary' and the 'Women's Wheel of Service'. In Clapham (1926) there was the 'Guild of Goodwill', and in Guildford (also 1926) the 'Ladies' Auxiliary of the Rotary Club'. Sunderland (1929) contented itself, like Norwich, with 'Ladies' Auxiliary', and Brixton (also 1929) was called the 'Guild of Service'.

By 1927 it was apparent, at least in the Lancashire area, that the rapidly multiplying Clubs needed co-ordination. There were by that time five other Clubs which had either started life as 'Inner Wheel' Clubs or adopted the name after establishment—namely Liverpool, Nelson, Macclesfield, St. Helens, and Warrington. These were all in No. 5 District of the Rotary organization (Lancashire and district), but they were already receiving enquiries from all parts of the United Kingdom. Accordingly, adopting the geographical arrangement of the Rotary Movement itself, they formed a 'No. 5 District Committee' to link the Clubs in that District and exchange views upon their policy and work. And in 1928 the Annual Conference of 'R.I.B.I.' (held at Harrogate) arranged, for the first time, a special session for women only. It was addressed by Mrs. Oliver Golding, who explained the purpose and organization of the 'Inner Wheel';

and a sequel to the occasion was that she was offered a monthly page in *The Rotary Wheel* as a medium for news of the women's Clubs. These events had resulted in the founding of twenty-nine more 'Inner Wheel' Clubs by the time the 1930 'R.I.B.I.' Conference assembled at Edinburgh, when the representatives of the thirty-five Clubs agreed to send the following resolution to their assembled men-folk :

(1) That women at this meeting respectfully ask R.I.B.I. to recognize the intense interest women associated with Rotarians take in all Rotary affairs and their anxiety to form units such as exist in No. 5 District.

(2) That this meeting would advise that all Clubs now formed, and those forming, be known by the uniform designation 'Inner Wheel'.

The reaction of the General Council of ' R.I.B.I.' was cautious, and non-committal. They were, perhaps, being asked to afford *de facto* recognition to a new phenomenon which they could not control. A little touched, maybe, at this formal acknowledgment of the women's need for their approval, they forbore to enquire too closely into the possible consequences, or indeed the ultimate utility, of withholding it. But they gave the ladies little encouragement.

However, the majority of the wives' Clubs, if they were not already called ' Inner Wheel ' Clubs, thereupon adopted the name and began to group themselves in Rotary ' Districts '; Districts 13 (Greater London) and 14 (Surrey and West Sussex) had ' Inner Wheel ' Committees by July 1931. By 1934 the Districts themselves were sufficiently numerous to need a central allegiance and direction; and the ' Association of Inner Wheel Clubs, Great Britain and Ireland ' came into existence, complete with a written Constitution (full of definitions and declarations) and ' Bye-laws ' for the proper conduct of Inner Wheel Clubs. Of this Association Mrs. Oliver Golding was elected the first President; and after two years of office, she was accorded the courtesy title of ' Founder-President ', so serving the Clubs in an advisory capacity until her death in 1938. The Constitution went annually through the same kind of vicissitudes as those which constantly beset the Constitution of ' R.I.B.I.', Rotarian wives displaying the same legislative zeal as their husbands. The changes reflected, in the main, various relaxations of the original rule that confined eligibility for ' Inner Wheel ' membership to wives of Rotarians, and one major change in status—the admission of overseas 'Inner Wheel' Clubs into the Association, which was in consequence renamed (in 1947) the 'Association of Inner Wheel Clubs', dropping any reference to nationality.

At the time of writing (1949), 'Inner Wheel' membership is of three classes—active, associate, and honorary. 'Active' membership is available to the wife of a Rotarian, to the widowed mother of a widower (or his daughter) or a bachelor Rotarian's widowed mother or widowed or single sister, and to a Rotarian's widow who applies to join a new Club in its first twelve months. 'Associate' membership brings in a Rotarian's unmarried (or widowed) daughter, and preserves the membership of the widowed mother of a bachelor Rotarian who marries. 'Honorary' members, of whom every Club is allowed two, need no qualification, whether of kinship or otherwise (and could, as the Constitution stands, include men!) Daughters must be over eighteen and, like mothers and sisters, must be members of a Rotarian's household.

Now, each of these refinements of dependency on the masculine stock is the result of some carefully-hatched amendment to the Constitution, designed as a rule to secure admission for some group of women excluded by the rigidity of the written word. Such cumulative, hair-splitting exactness is not traditionally British in origin, as we saw in the case of Rotary's behaviour at Conferences; but it may be an unavoidable result of organizing a club system on 'classification' lines. Other women's organizations (with the exception of the 'Soroptimists', a classification 'service' club for professional women, and an Anglo-American organization totally unconnected with the Rotary movement) have no such difficulties, and spend little time 'tinkering with the Constitution'. Rotarians and their ladies can never allow themselves to tire of it.

The objects of the 'Inner Wheel' are the same, *mutatis mutandis*, as those of the Rotary Movement. They meet either monthly or fortnightly, substituting 'true friendship' for 'fellowship' as 'an opportunity for service'; and they dedicate themselves to 'the betterment of social conditions'. They seek to 'promote a spirit of service among the womenfolk of Rotarians' (in which they assuredly succeed). They also set out to 'promote good international relations through the interchange of ideas', and in this, at least so far as concerns their sustained correspondence with Rotarians' wives overseas, they probably maintain a more vivid and lasting international relationship than do their husbands. They are gradually planting ' Inner Wheel ' Clubs in countries as diverse as Scandinavia, the Netherlands, Africa, Australia, Canada, and Malaya, and they have even begun infiltration into the United States, a re-export of the Rotary idea for which the existing American organization of ' Rotary-Annes ' appeared to leave little scope.

*   *   *   *   *

By December, 1949, there were over 500 ' Inner Wheel ' Clubs in Great Britain and Ireland, with over 14,000 members (as compared with Rotary's 650 Clubs and approximately 30,000 members); and ' extension ' was proceeding rapidly, the basis being that, wherever there was a Rotary Club which had actually received its ' charter ', there also should be its feminine counterpart—provided there were at least seven women willing to form a Club. A cautious misogyny showed itself, however, among many Rotarians. There was among the women a docile, though on the whole illusory, acknowledgment of vestigial male ascendancy in the fact that no Inner Wheel Club could be formed where the Rotary Club objected; and some of the Rotary Clubs did, occasionally with a vehemence that inadequately covered a note of defeatism. The right of veto was illusory in the eternal sense that women get what they want by making men want it first; and the men came to want it because so many of the ' Community Service ' activities of a Rotary Club depend for their fulfilment on the kind of services that women are best qualified to give—the provision and serving of refreshment at parties organized for children, for the poor, the crippled and the aged, the furnishing of hostels, the care of young children, etc. The women held it to be not only unnecessary but undesirable that the wife of the Rotary Club's president should be president of the ' Inner Wheel ' Club, and as time went on there were many obscure members of Rotary Clubs whose wives were national figures in the world of the ' Inner Wheel '. They bore this with fortitude.

Once established, every ' Inner Wheel ' Club was a completely autonomous unit, so that in addition to co-operation with the Rotary Club it undertook numerous welfare activities on its own account. It was only in its earliest days that the Movement functioned as an auxiliary to the Rotary Movement. Many canteens were established by Inner Wheel Clubs in the out-patients' departments of large hospitals, and car services were provided for poor women and children to and from hospitals and clinics. Service in day nurseries and crêches, in poor children's holiday centres, in girls' clubs, and in citizens' advice bureaux claimed the allegiance of many members. Others visited bed-ridden and blind people, and particularly those aged people living alone who, because they belonged to the 'middle classes', were erroneously thought by other organizations to be free from worries or the need for help and friendship. Others ran instruc-tional classes for unemployed women and handicraft classes for crippled children. Probation work and 'after-care' in the case of young offenders were regarded as no less important than prison-visiting.

* * * * *

Membership fees mounted as the structure of the Movement developed, from a shilling or two per annum in 1923 to as much as 30s. in 1949. The fact that, in the average domestic budgeting system, this money came out of the male pocket was never a serious reason for such male opposition as the Inner Wheel Movement encountered: ways and means are more important than emancipation. But the *ad hoc* subscriptions to this and that mainly feminine cause, the expenses at 'Inner Wheel' Con-ferences (which, as in the case of Rotary Conference expenses, were frequently not claimed from the official funds), and an occasional divergence of fireside opinion about the adequacy of a joint donation to a Rotary project—all these lent a gentle em-phasis to the fact that although an 'Inner Wheel' Club was a 'classification' club, the classification was that of the husband.

Yet by the nineteen-forties the Movement was too powerful to be other than a national institution in its own right. It was so acknowledged in public affairs; and it was represented on public bodies like the Women's Group on Public Welfare, local Councils of Social Service, the Women's Voluntary Services, the Women's Advisory Council of U.N.A., the Old People's Welfare Com-mittee, and the Economic Information Unit. It is sometimes said that the Movement grew out of the restlessness of women

K

who had accompanied their menfolk to week-end Rotary Conferences, where they found that a desire for active participation
survived even the lavish mannequin parades and other entertainments sometimes put on for their exclusive benefit.   It may be
so.   'The world owes its onward impulse', said Nathaniel
Hawthorne, ' to people ill at ease.'

*   *   *   *   *

II. The Round Table

Rotary's exclusion of any man who was not, at the least, in an
' executive position ' in his job was as restrictive as its rigid
limitation to ' two of a trade '.   On the whole, it kept out the
men under forty; and, as may be judged from the story of the
University settlements (to cite only one example), it is from men
much younger than forty that society has usually drawn its most
fervent enthusiasts for social service.

Rotarians were, almost from the beginning, uncomfortably
aware of this; but they also believed that their ' classification '
system was the foundation of their Movement's success, that
membership must be kept within limits, and that in particular
they should recruit men who could associate in the Clubs without
financial embarrassments.   They found no formula that would
overcome this dilemma in the Rotary Clubs themselves.   The
solution, when it came, was as inevitable as it was welcome.

It was an under-forty Rotarian, Louis Marchesi of the Norwich
Club, who provided it.   On 14th March, 1927, he called together
a group of the younger men of Norwich to discuss the formation
of a classification and service club for men under forty, and in
due course they formed the first ' Round Table '.   The vague
suggestion of identity with the chivalry of King Arthur's Knights
is due to the Movement's adoption of a phrase used by the Prince
of Wales in opening the British Industries Fair in 1927.   ' The
young business and professional men of this country,' he said,
' must get together *round the table*, adopt methods that have
proved so sound in the past, adapt them to the changing needs
of the time and, whenever possible, improve them."   The young
men of the new Movement chose ' Adopt, Adapt, Improve ' as
their motto, and (as an afterthought a few years later) sur-

mounted their circular badge with a replica of the legendary King Arthur.

In May, 1928, a clergyman of the Halifax Rotary Club, the Rev. J. L. Hines, read to the Annual Conference of R.I.B.I. a paper on 'What can Rotary do for the Younger Generation?' The 1914 war, he said, had claimed the ripe manhood of its day and left us with a generation of children. These had become the manhood of 1928, and they were 'characterized by a bold and assertive idealism, curiously mingled with an instinctive uncertainty concerning the true aims and ends of life'. He deplored Rotary's attitude of detachment to them, and urged the 'establishment of a junior affiliated society to Rotary throughout Britain'. Louis Marchesi, who spoke next, therefore surprised him (and most of the others) when he announced the existence of the Norwich Round Table, which now had ninety-six members. Portsmouth also had a Round Table, said Marchesi, with a membership of eighty. An early reluctance in the new Movement to accept any status as a kind of 'junior Rotary Club Movement' appeared in Marchesi's assurance to the assembled Rotarians that the Round Table movement 'asked only one thing of Rotary—its interest in the furtherance of the spirit of service'.[1] And the Conference resolved to 'foster the promotion, wherever possible, of Clubs of young business and professional men on lines similar to those actuating the Norwich Round Table Club'.

A fortnight later, on 25th May, 1928, the 'National Association of Round Tables of Great Britain and Ireland' was formed at a meeting at Rotary headquarters in London, by representatives from the only two such Clubs in existence—a gesture of confidence in the future of the new Movement which events were fully to justify. When the National Council of this Association met for the second time, on 4th October in the same year, six Clubs (they were already known as 'Tables') were represented ; Guildford, Southampton, Bournemouth, and Reading having followed the first two in that chronological order. Today (December, 1949) there are in Great Britain and Ireland 227 'Tables' and 6,500 members; and in comparing this with Rotary's respective figures of 668 and 30,000, it must be remembered that Rotary is the elder by sixteen years. Rotarians (many of whom are members of Round Table as well as of Rotary

[1] R.I.B.I. Conference *Proceedings*, 1928, p. 20.

Clubs) have done much to initiate and foster the Clubs in the newer Movement; and probably its most effective patron among Rotary leaders was Arthur Chadwick, President of R.I.B.I. in 1929, who was able to tell the 1929 R.I.B.I. Conference that fourteen more Round Tables had been formed in his year of office. A resolution of thanks to Chadwick, passed by the National Conference of 'Round Table' at Norwich on 3rd April, 1929, was proposed in a speech that likened the relationship between Rotary and Round Table to that between father and son —'the latter with an inclination to develop new ideas, and the former more cautious in such development, but both having the same ultimate object in view'. The father and son analogy is less apt today, the two organizations working on terms more closely resembling equality, and 'Round Table' having a carefully-drawn Constitution and Rules which differ in some fundamental respects from those of Rotary, not to mention a totally different system of territorial division.

There are many reasons for this. The Movement is *completely* autonomous, as are the Clubs within the Movement. Its relationship with the 'Round Table International', established in 1947 as a bond of international friendship once the Movement had spread to Europe and South Africa, is voluntary and ideological, not administrative; it is not tied to an international Constitution. Its liaison, through the ' World Council of Young Men's Service Clubs', with similar organizations abroad (the Kinsmen's Clubs of Canada, the Twenty-Thirty Clubs of the U.S.A. and Mexico, the 'Active' Clubs of the U.S.A. and Canada, the Apex Clubs of Australia) is also voluntary and harmonious, entailing no subordination of its original plans and ideas. Membership of 'Round Table' is far cheaper than membership of Rotary (though admittedly a financial strain on some of its younger members). 'Classification' requires merely that a member, who must be between eighteen and forty years old, shall be 'actually engaged in a business or profession, as principal or in a responsible position, or articled to a profession, or serving a properly indentured term of apprenticeship'; the ideal being that he shall be so engaged in a capacity that enables him to 'speak with authority upon his own vocation'. Four men from identical jobs may belong to the same 'Table'. Meetings in many of the Clubs are fortnightly rather than weekly, which simplifies the

' attendance ' problem—and, moreover, the meeting is often held after business hours in the evening; both these circumstances are important to men whose business and professional positions, though responsible, may be subordinate. The ' attendance rule ' requires only 50 per cent of possible attendances (as compared with Rotary's 60 per cent). And a man who moves to a new District may (with permission) transfer to a new ' Table ', although it may already have its constitutional quota of four men in his particular classification. (This latter concession did not come into operation until 1931; for some time it was opposed on the ground that ' more than 50 per cent of the members were professional men ', and that, ' since banking and insurance members were the ones who most frequently changed their addresses, some Clubs would be overstocked with them '. It was, however, decided upon as a means to eliminate abuses of the classification rule.)

The ' Round Tablers ' set out their aims and objects thus :

(1) To develop the acquaintance of young men through the medium of their professional and business occupations. (2) To emphasize the fact that one's calling offers an excellent medium of service to the Community. (3) To cultivate the highest ideals in business, professional, and civic traditions. (4) To recognize the worthiness of all legitimate occupations, and to dignify each his own by precept and example. (5) To further the establishment of peace and goodwill in international relationships. And (6) to further the above objects by meetings, lectures, discussions, and other activities.

These had a familiar Rotary sound. Numbers 2, 3 and 4, which are almost universal in ' service ' clubs, could remain valid only so long as the eligible ' qualifications ' (which ' Round Table ' catalogued with some care, though without the immense prolixity of the Rotary *Outline of Classifications*) remained ' respectably ' exclusive. Number 5 was to be implemented by ' maintaining contact with kindred organizations ' abroad, which may well be considered a sensible and modest programme unclouded by vague aspirations and woolly pronouncements. And number 6 was almost too modest : the ' Round Tablers ' initiated many ' other activities ' which were not at all *ejusdem generis* with ' meetings, lectures, and discussions '—their work for the young and the old, for the helpless and the crippled, co-ordinated in every Club by a Community Service Committee, could be

accepted by all but the sourest cynic as in itself a justification of the
entire organization.

The Second World War, with its demands on man-power of
' Round Table ' age, almost resulted in the eclipse of the Movement in this country. Over two-thirds of its members left
the ' active ' list for service in the Forces, and many of the
remainder were engaged on duties that made attendance at their
Clubs impossible. The headquarters office in London was
closed, control of the Movement was vested in an Executive
Committee, and the age limit of forty was suspended. But at the
end of hostilities the full machinery was set up again, and from
1946 onwards the recovery was spectacular.

It was an arbitrary rule that every man's membership ceased
on the 31st March following his fortieth birthday. True, there
was a possibility that he might, if his services to the club or its
social service interests were thought to have been especially
distinguished, be made an honorary member—and perhaps re-
elected as such for two or three successive years; but it was a
high honour reserved for the few. Such a rule inevitably meant
that men of thirty-five and over showed a reluctance to join that
increased as they neared the disqualifying age, and brought the
average age to something below thirty. A ' Round Table ' was
in no sense an ante-room to Rotary membership, nor did it in the
smallest degree increase the eligibility of a man (though it might
enhance his acceptability) for Rotary membership : the utmost
that it might do was to predispose him to accept an invitation
to Rotary membership if it came his way. This might even
happen while he was still under forty and a member of ' Round
Table '; but it was much more likely, by the law of averages,
that it would never happen at all. If, however, you are to have a
club for young men, you must fix an age at which a man is to be
deemed no longer young. As the number of age-disqualified ex-
members increased, so did the likelihood that they would form
some kind of association for the excluded; and in 1937, accordingly,
there began (at Liverpool) the formation of ' 41-clubs ', otherwise
known as ' Ex-Tablers' Clubs '. By December, 1949, there were
eighteen of these affiliated to a ' National Association of Ex-
Tabler Clubs ', and there were yet others which preferred to remain unaffiliated. Genuinely ' clubbable men ' will not remain
long asunder.

Nor, it seems, will their womenfolk. From Rotary came the ' Inner Wheel ': from Round Table came—the ' Ladies' Circle '. Formed in 1933 within a few weeks of each other by the wives (and wives only) of ' Round Tablers ', the first two ' Ladies' Circles '—at Manchester and Bournemouth—had in six years been emulated in a sufficient number of towns to warrant the formation of yet another national Movement—the ' National Association of Ladies' Circles ', to which in December, 1949, thirty-seven ' Circles ' were affiliated. Among themselves, their members gently exploited the fount of friendship to the considerable benefit of local charities, and they co-operated with their husbands' Clubs in the organization of entertainments, fêtes, and outings to a similar purpose. It may be imagined that, as with members of the ' Inner Wheel ' and their Rotarian menfolk, the wives in the ' Ladies' Circles ' were early aware of the strain on household funds of this dual membership in service clubs; and that, since ' Round Tablers ' were for the most part men with lower incomes than Rotarians, the strain in their case was the more severe. But the women of this auxiliary Movement were not to be denied or discouraged. The Movement grew rapidly; and when this book was going to press, they had just discussed at their Association's sixth Annual General Meeting whether their members should be subject, like their husbands, to a retirement rule based on a maximum age. Decision on this point was postponed; and it is at once the strength and refuge of the historian, whose work is to present an unemotional picture of the past, that his terms of reference preclude (or at least discourage) any impious peeps into the future.

Chapter Thirteen

THE CRITICS

' To accuse ', said Thomas Hobbes in *Leviathan*, ' requires less eloquence, such is man's nature, than to excuse; and condemnation, more than absolution, resembles justice.'

Has the Rotary Movement had justice from its critics ? Whatever is prominent or different will attract criticism; but it is not enough to say of this Movement that the critics, prompted merely by cynicism, will find hypocrisy behind every appearance of good; it is certainly not enough to say that, being outside the Movement, they are moved by envy or the malevolent curiosity of the excluded (though some of them are). Their curiosity may be easily sated. The Rotary Club is in no sense a secret society, its meetings are attended (on invitation) by non-Rotarians, its proceedings are reported in the Press, its literature may be read by all. It is noteworthy, in relation to a Movement which has evolved an otherwise perfect formula for unshakable *bonhomie*, that its most cogent and bitter critics are within its own ranks. Ah, but do they mean, or do they even think they mean, what they say ? If not, their vehemence in saying it to each other could be explained only by the psycho-analyst. Every relevant criticism, at least of the Rotary manifestation in Great Britain and Ireland, is to be found in the correspondence pages of its monthly journal; impatient, angry, embarrassed and heretical letters from men who were nauseated by such seemingly innocuous phrases as ' the spirit of Rotary ', ' Service above Self ', and ' he profits most who serves best '. There, in the files of their journal, they stand in their hundreds, these protests from men who wanted their Movement to keep its feet on the ground, ephemeral protests now lost to all but the historian who violates their cramped and silent immortality. Consider these few examples of what they have said.

Where there has been a clash of principles, Rotary has shirked the issue or expressed itself in sonorous phrases. It has gloried in its aim to promote understanding, but has been afraid to be plain-spoken for fear of hurting the other fellow. (A Rotarian clergyman addressing a neighbouring Club.)

We have feared to say too much for fear of giving offence. We have searched for phrases to express our case which left the back door open for retreat if they gave offence. It is exceedingly difficult for a large international organisation to pilot its faith through the ramifications of varying political and economic expressions. Nevertheless that is Rotary's declared duty. (A Past-President of the Association, writing in *Rotary Service* during the Second World War.)

Rotary encourages service for any and every purpose in any and every direction. Its members stand for contrary and conflicting ideals, and it necessarily follows that the movement, as a movement, stands for exactly nothing at all. (A Rotarian addressing his own Club.)

I gave two days a week for two years to Rotary and came out of office a very sadly disillusioned man. There are far too many Rotarians who do not one single thing for the movement except to attend a lunch weekly. (A District Past-Chairman in a letter to *The Rotary Wheel*.)

Rotary is like a child who listens to the arguments of the learned and then returns to his play, oblivious of all he has heard. Rotary has not grown up. As now constituted it never can grow up. It can only spread. (A letter in a Club Bulletin.)

We have all heard speakers lay stress on Rotary's immense possibilities for good, their argument being based on our high ideals. And our membership is strong and of some quality. If these two mated to create action, then Rotary would be the vital, living, worth-while force we sometimes pretend that it is. But until action is born of the union, Rotary will remain little more than a good club, rich in fellowship but of little real effect in the world at large. (A letter to *The Rotary Wheel*.)

Is there not maybe too much rushing around by a small group of Super-Rotarians, fruitless rushing around, the cost of which, if spent on really constructive work, might almost be enough to transform the world? . . . The time is overdue for our vast movement to prove itself to be more than a tourist agency or a holiday association. (A Rotarian—a Labour M.P.—in an article in *The Rotary Wheel*.)

Please tell us what bearing the continuous chanting of glad hosannas at pleasant watering-places has upon the ethics of Rotary. (Letter to *The Rotary Wheel* from a Rotarian who doubted the value of the Conferences.)

How far do the members know anything about what is coming on at the Conference? This has been my experience again this year: a week before the Conference the Club President announces that he has received fifteen resolutions which are to be submitted at the Conference. Shall he read them ? Shouts of ' No ' from the luncheon tables. Why ? There is an honoured guest who has been invited to address the Club. Members want to hear him. (Letter to *The Rotary Wheel*.)

Recently, while discussing the ethics of Rotary with a non-Rotarian friend residing in a Midland town, I was given with assurance the information that several Rotarians in that town had confessed, in private conversation, that their association with Rotary was purely a matter of business, and that they asked for and expected that trading preferences should be given to them by fellow members. (Letter to *The Rotary Wheel*.)

The ' Spend for Employment ' Scheme (see page 107) is the first thing I have seen that has given me the slightest hope that Rotary may ever do any good. There has been a definite attempt to give a lead, and Rotarians have worked for an end, not to get themselves and the movement into the limelight. (Letter from the Past-President of a Club to *The Rotary Wheel*.)

Who is going to take the next step to relieve Rotary of much of the junk, much of the stuff and nonsense which in my opinion is spoiling it, and preventing it doing automatically maybe all or even more than is being asked by the powers that be ? It did wonderful work through Clubs and individual members in the past when it was allowed to do it for its own pleasure and out of its own creation, but to-day it is being ' school-boyed ' into doing things unwillingly or not at all. . . . Can we not go back to the simple Rotary ? (Letter from a club secretary to *The Rotary Wheel*.)

There is too much machinery, and this machinery has a deadening influence. Its noise confuses the poor average Club member; its literature sends him to sleep. (Letter to *The Rotary Wheel*.)

Take a bottle of stout and give it a good shaking-up; and then uncork. You will get nothing but froth. Rotary is like that. (Letter to *The Rotary Wheel*.)

All these criticisms evoked their answers from the faithful, but the reader may perhaps form his own judgment upon them from the pages of this book. The angry recipe at the end has not been surpassed in pungent brevity by anything said of Rotary in Britain or America; but it was said by a Rotarian who, having the furtherance of his Movement at heart, felt that it was stultified by the competitive struggle for 100 per cent Club attendances and the award of prizes and ' honourable mentions ', by exhortations to Community Service that took from it the joy of spontaneity, and in particular by injunctions that the Clubs should ' get to know their towns ' by conducting detailed ' civic surveys '. But a similar vein of criticism runs through all the extracts quoted, which may be regarded as evidence that docility is not a necessary feature of Rotary membership.

Rotarians in this country have been able to feel that the most scorching indictments of the Movement have been written by Americans, for Americans, about the American aspect of Rotary. Sinclair Lewis left them unscathed when he wrote in his 1934 book *A Work of Art* that ' a Boy Scout is a young Rotarian and a Rotarian is a Boy Scout in long trousers ', because in this country the Scout Movement carries over from childhood to maturity with a kind of nostalgic dignity. With his powerful admixture of savage irony and lapses into tenderness, Lewis portrayed in *Babbitt* what he conceived to be the typical real estate agent combining ruthless money-making with a kind of pop-eyed joviality in membership of a typical ' service club '. But Zenith, where George Babbitt lived and loved and fretted and cheated, was in America. And one knew that the American citizen at play was an incitement to derision in American non-players, who were at least in a position to understand the game; whilst American business probity might have different bases. . . . The picture did not, it was with some justification maintained, portray the typical Rotarian in this country, and American Rotarians were well able to look after themselves.

It was for them also to bear with H. L. Mencken, who peppered his satirical comments on contemporary man with an occasional drop of venom for Rotarians; but in this country the Movement was not unaware of him. ' A great deal of cant has, of course, been talked about " Service ",' says the R.I.B.I. Pamphlet *Synopsis of Rotary*, ' so much as almost to discredit the word entirely. Commerce has succeeded in prostituting it to the extent that its decent votaries are those who least frequently speak of it.' (This, perhaps, was harsh and a little embarrassing. It had decent votaries in the Movement who spoke of it at every meeting.) ' " As soon as a group of real-estaters get together and sob for Service," says Mencken somewhere, " somebody is going to be done. " What, then, does Rotary mean by the word? As briefly (and as absolutely) as possible, it means " something for nothing ". . . . It is a virtue of giving which is its own reward, carrying no intent of an ultimate return, moral or material.' To have no ' intent ' of moral comfort in beneficence would involve an introspection bordering on the metaphysical. But, goes on the pamphlet, 'the very consciousness of virtue in giving is virtue's imponderable reward, and such imponderables cannot humanly be eliminated. . . . Let us try to dismiss these attempts at definition by saying that Rotary regards service as the highest altruism of which a given individual is capable.' Rotarians, in fact, could defend themselves—but only amongst each other. Outside the Movement, not only was no one interested in the defence; no one wanted to hear it in case some of it might be true. This is a busy world; it likes simple judgments ready-made.

Rotarians had not, however, expected their Movement to be chosen as a windmill by that mighty Don Quixote, G. K. Chesterton. In full tilt during a public breakfast in New York in 1931, G.K.C. had this to declaim :

I do not dislike Rotarianism with the fury of H. L. Mencken or Sinclair Lewis, but I agree with them that it is a form of comradeship that is gross, common, vainglorious, blatant, sentimental and, in a word, caddish. . . . There is something vulgar about such companionship. It lacks spiritual dignity. Almost all people of sensitive instincts will be ready to agree that there has descended on all that sort of thing a something filled with the wind of self-advertisement. There is something caddish about it. The Church exists, among other things, to maintain the concept of human dignity in what may be called This Rotarian Age. Why is there this debasement of human friendship ? Because men were not meant to be sufficient to themselves or to each other. Two Rotarians complimenting each other are like two savages rubbing noses, compared with the great saints and heroes. . . . There is not mystery about a Rotary luncheon. There must be something of surprise, something of mystery, something of God in our relationships. Without the admiration of something better than ourselves or each other, we become a mutual admiration society and a very paltry collection of snobs.

A New York public breakfast was a comfortable distance away. But this was our own lusty Chesterton, who, to the joy of all but his victims, was always tearing the veil of pretence from some fallible institution over here, and exposing it to the clean sweet wind of publicity. His attack on Rotary made some members re-examine their motives. Many of them, perhaps a majority, were members of churches, even of the Catholic Church, in whose great cause G.K.C. was such a stentorian champion. There were few Clubs that did not contain members of the Clergy, and some had Bishops. The reeling Movement recovered. It noted Chesterton's refusal to dislike it with the fury of Mencken and Lewis, and found comfort in speculating how much worse it would be if he did. Persisting in their debasement of human friendship, Rotarians built more homes for slum-dwellers, busied themselves among the blind and the crippled, and released their idle capital to provide work for the unemployed in the world-wide depression that obstinately survived the oratory of great public breakfasts. Paul Harris called his next book *This Rotarian Age*.

They were, in short, irrepressible. In 1926 the Vicar of Leeds, the Rev. Canon W. Thompson Elliott, the previous year's President of 'R.I.B.I.', delighted them when he described in a Conference speech a satirical play about Rotary which he had just seen in New York. One of its scenes concerned the introduction of new members to a Rotary Club.

The Member who introduced them began in the usual Rotary way by saying that he was not a good speaker. The first one he had to introduce was so-and-so, and his classification was that of a crutch-tipper—he put the rubber tips on crutches. He was a good fellow, he had made good, had got both feet on the ground, and would make a good member of the club. The second man was a step-tacker; he tacked the advertisements on the steps at railway stations. He was a good fellow, had made good, had both feet on the ground, and would make a good member of the club. The third man was a moth-ball designer; he designed the round moth-ball. Previous to his great discovery moth-balls had been square. Since his remarkably ingenious invention more moth-balls had got lost, to the good of the moth-ball trade. He was a good fellow, had made good, had both feet on the ground, and would make a very good member of the club.

This kind of thing might suggest itself as Rotary's penalty for not maintaining secrecy about its domestic dispositions. But to most Rotarians in this country it is a source of unaffected joy. Whether their imperviousness reflects a healthy objectivity or a dull lack of sensitivity may afford grounds for debate; but the debaters should know their men. Each hypothesis could be a recipe for strength, but certain aspects of the strength which the Movement has displayed on this side of the Atlantic suggest objectivity.

Criticism in this country, which in the main has been cryptic and satirical, has sprung from the fact that anyone using the term 'business-man' is always being objective. He always means someone else, someone who gets his living differently and therefore, in all likelihood, unscrupulously. Wyndham Lewis (Timothy Shy of the *News Chronicle*) illustrates this:

Lunching with a gang of idealistic business-men the other day, we noted a new routine. Before the cry 'Service, Not Self!' was raised, all the doors were locked. The usual panic-rush of listeners to safety was thus made impossible. We didn't mind this so much as we minded the sardonic grins of the waiters.[1]

The idealistic business-man, that is to say, is either a fabulous monster or a blend of confidence trickster and fraudulent sidesman. In either case he is a figure of fun to be sustained with a kind of poetic licence, as when Timothy Shy again descended upon 'slightly woozy Rotarians singing "For He's a Jolly Good Fellow"'.[2] He serves a definite purpose in the zoology of social butts, and there is little relevance in the fact that, since the majority of Rotary lunches are teetotal, 'wooziness' must be invented to make them comic.

To the Olympian eye most gatherings of men are comic. To eavesdrop at a table where any four business-men met regularly for lunch, unless they were discussing the Government or agreeing the terms of a petition in bankruptcy, would in most cases be a disenchantment to anyone expecting near-Johnsonian discourse. But even if they were convicted of fatuity by this austere standard of judgment, it would be because they lacked a chairman, an agenda, and a purpose bigger than their foursome. The standard of conversation at Rotary lunches is not that of the Mermaid Tavern nor the pattern of behaviour that of the Court of St. James; but by getting formally together and giving themselves a name they have dared comparison, and they will get no more mercy than clergymen, lawyers, governments, trades unions, or flat-earthers.

Since we are concerned here solely with the Movement in Great Britain and Ireland, no consideration has been given to any criticisms voiced by American Rotarians of the Movement in its

[1] *News Chronicle*, 13th April, 1949.
[2] *News Chronicle*, 6th July, 1934.

American form. That these were somewhat negligible as recently as 1930 is apparent from Paul Harris's address to the Rotary Club of Chicago on the occasion of its twenty-fifth anniversary.

> Business [said Harris] employs its own critics—researchmen—and pays them munificent salaries. They probe into the vitals of great machines to detect their weaknesses, in order that they may condemn them. Rotary has no critics on its salaried list. They are all on the outside, and while their work is not without virtue, it is not without vice. Rotary needs a department for constructive criticism—something comparable to the research departments of great businesses.

In this country there is no need for Rotary to employ salaried critics, as the opening paragraphs of this chapter were designed to show. Perhaps this emphasizes as nothing else could that the Movement has, and is bound to have, national peculiarities. British members have set their faces against most of the organized high-jinks that have expressed the ebullient American personality *en masse*. As early as 1924 one member proposed that all the cars converging on the Torquay Conference should assemble outside the town, decorate themselves with flags, and drive in procession to their hotels; and the idea was turned down with shocked emphasis. There were men present who had seen American processions of decorated Rotarians marching behind a brass band.

Perhaps their worst critics do not accuse Rotarians of being Machiavellian, condemned by their own ethics to the hypocrisy of professing virtue and practising vice; and where they are accused of selfishness, it is as a rule because their accusers do not know the range of their activities. Selfishness, indeed, says Professor Barrows Dunham in discussing the thesis that ' You have to look after yourself ', is not ultimately a workable creed; though—

> The test of workability [he adds] will not finally decide the merits of social-mindedness as against selfishness. There is ill-success in the practice of both. We have got to face a much larger question, the question why the one is *better* than the other. We have to try to show that an act which benefits society, though it may injure the doer, is better than an act which injures society though it may benefit the doer.[1]

[1] *Man Against Myth*. Frederick Muller, Ltd., 1948. Page 183.

Inside or outside the Movement, well or ill informed, baleful or flippant, the critics will do it good if they keep before it the picture of its own difficult intentions.

*   *   *   *   *

So far as it can truly be called a constructive international ideology, the future of the Rotary Club Movement seems assured. It is true that two-thirds of its Clubs are still to be found in the United States, where, forty-five years ago, the Rotary Club of Chicago was destined for three years to be the only such Club in the world; but there are now nearly 7,000 scattered throughout every continent. The future of 'Rotary International' as an administrative entity is less predictable. The prospect is clouded by a strange conflict of loyalties in a world whose inter-State contacts have for upwards of thirty years been those of belligerents in global warfare. There is an advocacy of world-Government side by side with the growing parochialism that leads to secession from empires and the compulsory training of children to talk moribund dialects. As a reaction against a growing neighbourliness, there are vast areas of the earth where the leaders of men believe, with Rémy de Gourmont, that ' it is because peoples do not know each other that they hate each other so little '. There is still a disturbing possibility, despite the eclipse of Fascism and National Socialism, that, in their anxiety to defeat the newer totalitarianism, the lovers of liberty may destroy the thing they love. A world of armed absolutism would make short work of Rotary and its kindred universalisms. The first Rotary Club on the European continent was established (in 1921) in Madrid, but there are no Rotary Clubs in Spain to-day; nor are there any now beyond the Iron Curtain. In order to discuss the future of ' R.I.B.I.', one must make large and confident assumptions.

Assuming, therefore, that what is now called ' representative democracy ' either wins the battle for men's minds, or by compromise averts the battle for their bodies, there can be little doubt that the Movement, gaining strength and recognition as a social service organization of importance, will retain and develop strong national characteristics. In Great Britain and Ireland these characteristics, as compared with those of the American membership, will probably consist mainly in things that the British will not do rather than those which they will do, in an increasingly decorous purposefulness rather than any growth of hot-gospel ostentation. The familiar criticism that ' Community Service ' contents itself with palliation, and accepts without effective challenge the causes of what it palliates, will remain as true of the Rotary movement as of the Church, the judiciary and the voluntary charities. There is no escape from the quandary that, in the modern 'Welfare State', the treatment of causes is a political undertaking, and that Rotary could attack them only by entering the political arena—at the very least as a ' pressure group '.

This would kill the Movement by splitting the Clubs; for although the Club members are overwhelmingly right-wing in political thinking, a high proportion of them are less right-wing than the fervid apologists of modern British Conservatism, which they regard as an unconstructive reaction against Socialism. Even Conservative business-men, who are usually ahead of the professional politician in their comprehension of industrial problems, are sometimes dismayed at the die-hardism they observe in the extremes of the party they support. Meanwhile, however, an administrative solution must be found for the problem presented to the Clubs by the nationalization of staple industries and welfare services, and the losses of Club membership due to consequent removals and changes of personal status. There appears to be little substance in the belief that the scope for voluntary social service will ever be entirely abolished by government paternalism.

Changes in the rules as to eligibility for membership do not seem as important to the spread of the Movement as the would-be Rotarian is apt to assert. There is probably no Club in the country with all its ' classifications ' filled, and few which could not fill most of their vacancies from available and suitable men in their territory. The need for this kind of ' extension ', even in preference to the formation of new Clubs, is a constant theme in the injunctions issued from headquarters to the Clubs. But the possibilities of new formations are far greater than the present slow rate of expansion would suggest, particularly in the large provincial cities, where the existing Clubs, already too large for convenient administration or intimate acquaintance among their members, could certainly throw open portions of their territory for the formation of new Clubs without themselves foregoing any recruiting rights therein, as has been done in London.

L

An immediate problem of urgency, however, is the future of
the Annual Conference of 'R.I.B.I.' In 1949, over 5,000 people
attended the Conference at Blackpool, of whom more than
2,000 were the wives and daughters of Rotarians present. Blackpool and Bournemouth are the only towns in Great Britain and
Ireland capable of satisfactorily accommodating so large a number
of visitors in their hotels (the Conference lasts for four days) and
in their conference halls. To hold the Conference at these two
towns in alternate years would be to distribute unfairly the incon-
veniences of travel and length of absence from home and business,
besides being a considerable strain on the Rotary Clubs of those
towns, upon which fall certain duties of hospitality as 'host
clubs'. Yet the annual change of scene, from 1921 onwards,
through Edinburgh, Margate, Torquay, Bournemouth, Scar-
borough, Douglas, Llandudno, and so on, was possible only by
reason of the smaller Conferences of those years. Moreover, the
huge number of 'voting delegates' attending the main business
conference, at which the Resolutions and amendments from the
Clubs were put to the vote, belied their appearance of strength
through the well-known procedural paradox that numerical force
'on the floor' facilitates demagogic guile on the platform. There
were less than thirty men on the platform, comprising mainly the
General Council. A similar number of resolute and articulate
men 'on the floor' could be difficult to manage and perhaps, on
controversial issues, impossible to convince. The 'management' of 1,500 men was, by comparison, simple.

Yet, though democratic principles were in theory fulfilled and
the very word 'democracy' was almost the pass-word of the
occasion, many of those present knew that they had lost the
substance of democracy by a mass pursuit of its shadow. The
'sovereign power' which the Clubs were supposed to exercise
through their voting delegates (two from each Club) was diminish-
ing as the size of the Conferences grew. A Resolution was
announced to the assembled thousands by the President of the
year (as Chairman of the 'business session'), using a microphone.
Its proposer and seconder spoke in support of it, followed by
proposers and seconders of amendments to it, all using extra
microphones, placed below the platform, and speaking for a permitted maximum of minutes. They were followed in turn by
their opponents and supporters. There might well be hundreds

present with something cogent to say on the subject, but there was a long agenda to work through, and in the offing there was lunch or tea for the 5,000. No one was discouraged by the 'chair' from contributing to the debate, but many were discouraged by hunger, discomfort, or the loss of personal significance that afflicts the individual engulfed by numbers.

But the full-scale Annual Conference, with its concomitant social functions and its opportunities for renewing numerous acquaintanceships, is an institution which the Movement will not lightly forgo. It is cherished as a source of 'inspiration'. In 1949 a plan was devised for two kinds of Conference, to be held in alternate years. The first would be a 'delegate conference' for the transaction of legislative matters and financial business, limited to one voting delegate from each Club and totalling, with the 'officers' of the Movement and a proposed 'Council on Legislation', about 1,000 men. Even so, each Rotarian would be entitled to bring one lady with him; but this was expected, on a basis of experience, to produce an aggregate of not more than 1,500 people which could be accommodated at a reasonable variety of suitable towns. The second would be an 'open' Conference of the kind which Rotarians call 'social and inspirational' and was expected to go on reaching the now customary figure of 5,000. The probability that this would, at no very distant date, become impossible to accommodate anywhere in the country was regarded as less disturbing than the fact that the 'delegate conference', unless held as an entirely separate occasion, would share its fate.

The work of the 'delegate conference', under this plan, was to be reduced by a system of 'filtering' Club Resolutions at District level. A Resolution approved by a District Council would go forward to a newly-constituted 'Council on Legislation', composed of four elected men from each of the eighteen Districts and certain of the Officers of the Movement, to a total of eighty-five men. This would be entrusted with the work of eliminating Resolutions which, because they were *ultra vires* or frivolous or based on a complete misunderstanding of some enactment which they sought to amend, would waste the time of the 'delegate conference'. But any Club which felt aggrieved at the rejection of its submitted Resolution was to retain the right to carry it right through to the 'delegate conference', and there let it take its

chance at the hands of the ' voting delegates ' as a measure that
had already been condemned both by a District Council and by the
Council on Legislation.

Although a similar scheme had already been adopted by the
' International ' for the purposes of world Conventions, the
delegates at the 1949 Conference of ' R.I.B.I.' were not ready
for it; and after a ' floor-*versus*-platform ' struggle which produced some lively controversy, the delegates, with the blessed
relief of procrastination, put it off for a year, and hoped that their
distraught Conference Committee would find some way of staging
at least one more mammoth Conference. It was later decided to
hold this, the 1950 Conference, at Bournemouth; but meanwhile
a partial (and on the whole unpopular) solution presented itself.
This was the joint decision of the governing bodies of ' R.I.B.I.'
and the ' Inner Wheel ' to separate the women's conference—
and hold it in another town. When this book went to press it
seemed inevitable that the plan for a ' delegate ' and ' open '
Conference in alternate years must sooner or later be accepted;
but for the time being, owing to opposition from the Clubs, all
that survived of it was the principle that Club Resolutions for the
Conference should be submitted to District Councils for ' vetting ',
with the right to proceed against that Council's decision if the
Club insisted.

Consideration of ' R.I.B.I.'s ' future must raise in any critical
mind the position of the Association's ' past-Presidents '. Each
man who has held the highest office in the Movement has had
five years of intimate concern with its administration—one at
least as Rotary International Representative, and one as Vice-
President, as President, as ' immediate Past-President ', and as the
representative on the Board of Rotary International of the Clubs
in this country. Thereafter, he resumes the status of an ordinary
Club member, except that he automatically becomes for life a
member of a ' Past Presidents' Advisory Committee '. This is
accordingly a body of experienced men past middle age, numbering
perhaps twelve at any one time and depleted only by the deaths
of its members, which comprises the ' elder statesmen ' of the
Association. The value of its accumulated experience is incomparable. But, for the most part, it is wasted. It can merely
offer suggestions, which the General Council and the voting
delegates at Conferences can (and do) disregard. It is not the

part of the historian to proffer suggestions for the future; but supposing the development of ' R.I.B.I.' to have an individual future reflecting the British rather than the American democratic system, it would be surprising if some way were not eventually found of integrating the Past Presidents' Committee into the legislative machinery of the Association. There may be an analogy in the position of the Privy Council, since, although the Association cannot be likened to a constitutional monarchy, it could pass ' skeleton ' statutes to be implemented by Orders in Council. It may be more apt to visualize the Past Presidents' Committee as a ' second chamber ', with power to initiate legislation for the approval of the ' lower house ', though the right to veto legislation originating in the lower house would need safeguards that might well perplex the draughtsmen of any ' Parliament Bill ' at Westminster. It is an interesting line of thought for those concerned with the future of the Movement.

Whatever new forms the Movement may adopt, that future is assured so long as democracy, State paternalism, and small-scale business enterprise continue to be rationally accepted as compatibles, and so long as men can feel themselves emotionally enriched by associating under rules that inhibit vital controversy. In Great Britain and Ireland, moreover, even if in no other country where it has taken root, the fate of the Rotary Movement is linked with the future of the middle classes, whose particular century this once promised to be. And if there is one century which interests contemporary citizens more than the twentieth, it is the twenty-first. The future is more worth working for than the present : there is so much more of it.

BIBLIOGRAPHY

BOOKS

Babbitt. By Sinclair Lewis. Jonathan Cape, 1934.

This Rotarian Age. By Paul Harris. Rotary International (Chicago). 1935.

Rotary? A University Group Looks at the Rotary Club of Chicago. University of Chicago Press. 1934.

Rotary and its Brothers: an Analysis and Interpretation of the Men's Service Club. By Charles F. Marden. Princeton University Press. 1935.

My Road to Rotary. By Paul Harris. Kroch & Son, Chicago. 1949.

The Meaning of Rotary. By a Rotarian. 'R.I.B.I.' 1927.

Spotlights on Rotary. By William Moffatt. Wm. Walker & Sons (Otley) Ltd. 1947.

The Romance of Rotary in London. By Vivian Carter. Rotary International in Great Britain and Ireland, District 13. 1947.

Service is My Business. Anonymous. Rotary International (Chicago). 1948.

Rotary Studies in Reconstruction. Rotary International in Great Britain and Ireland. 1945.

The Common People. By G. D. H. Cole and Raymond Postgate. Methuen. 1938.

English Social History. By G. M. Trevelyan. Longmans, Green & Co. 1944.

The English Middle Classes. By Roy Lewis and Angus Maude. Phoenix House. 1949.

Man Against Myth. By Barrows Dunham. Frederick Muller, Ltd. 1948.

PAMPHLETS, ETC.

Rotary International 'Constitution and By-laws'. (R.I., Chicago).

'R.I.B.I.' Constitution and By-laws.

'R.I.B.I.' Standard Club Constitution and By-laws.

Synopsis of Rotary. 'R.I.B.I.', various editions.

Outline of Classifications. (R.I., Chicago, with an 'R.I.B.I.' Supplement). 1949.

Rotary—Its History, Its Interpretation, and Its Possibilities. By Thomas Stephenson. British Association of Rotary Clubs. 1923.

How to Form a Rotary Club. 'R.I.B.I.' 1948.

Club Service
Community Service   } 'R.I.B.I.', various editions.
Vocational Service
International Service

Guide to Club Executives ⎫ 'R.I.B.I.', various editions.
Guide to District Executives ⎭

Combined Operations. 'R.I.B.I.' 1946.
Summary of Evidence. 'R.I.B.I.' 1949.
Towards European Unity. 'R.I.B.I.' 1948.
The Public v. *The Slums.* 'R.I.B.I.' 1933.
Youth. 'R.I.B.I.' 1937.
Youth Travel Guide. 'R.I.B.I.' 1937.
Monetary Systems and Theories. By G. D. H. Cole. 'R.I.B.I.' 1943.

PERIODICALS, ETC.

Proceedings of Rotary International Conventions, 1921 to 1949. Rotary International (Chicago).
Proceedings of 'R.I.B.I.' Conferences, 1924 to 1949.
Reports from 'R.I.B.I.' District Chairmen.
Reports of Club Secretaries' Conferences.
The Rotary Wheel, monthly, 1915 to 1942. ('R.I.B.I.') (Under title *Rotary,* 1925–6.)
Rotary Service, every two months, 1942–7, monthly 1947–9. ('R.I.B.I.')
Service in Life and Work. Quarterly, 1932 to 1939. ('R.I.B.I.')
The Rotarian. R.I., Chicago. Monthly, 1920 to 1949.

INDEX

A

ABERDEEN, Rotary Club of, 21
Active Members, 66
Addison, Joseph, 15, 16
Additional Active Members, 66
Administration :
    Area, 48, 52, 53, 55
    District, 48
    National, 48
    Rotary International Commission on, 54
    Territorial, 48, 55
Advertising by Rotarians, 30
Aims and Objects Committees, 28
Aims and Objects Plan, the, 34, 53, 59, 62, 78, 92
Air-raid Distress Funds, 125
Alexander, W. H., 53
Allied troops, entertainment of, 129
Annual Conference of R.I.B.I., the, 46
    criticism of, 145
    future of, 154
    resolutions to, 154, 155
    voting delegates to, 154
Archdale, Mrs., 132
Area Administration, 48, 52, 53, 55
Arts Council of Great Britain, the, 109
Assembly :
    Club, 36
    District, 33, 34, 35
    ' National ', 35
Associate Members, 65
Associates for Anglo-American Understanding, 131
Astor, Lady, 132
Attendance Rule, the, 6, 71
    Committee, 71
    objections to 25, 68, 146
' Auxiliary to the Rotary Club ', the, 133

B

Babbitt, 24, 147
Bantam Battalions, the, 31
Belfast, Rotary Club of, 17, 18, 89
Beveridge Plan, the, 124
Bevin, Ernest, 123
Birmingham, Rotary Club of, 17, 18, 41, 125
Blackburn, Rotary Club of, 87
Blackpool as Conference centre, 154

Blackpool Conference, the, 1936, 84; 1949, 154
Bliven, Bruce, 74
Block Grant, the, 36
Board of Directors of B.A.R.C., 21
    of R.I.B.I., 54
Borstal Association, the, 102
Bournemouth, as Conference centre, 154
Bournemouth Conference, the, 1950, 156
Bournemouth, Rotary Club of, 101
Boy Scouts, the, 101, 118
Boys' Camps, 101
Boys' Clubs, 101
Bribery and Secret Commissions Prevention League, 80
Bribery, Rotary attitude to, 28, 45, 80, 82, 83, 119
Bristol Little Theatre, 107
Bristol, Rotary Club of, 21, 100, 107, 108
British Association of Rotary Clubs (' B.A.R.C.'), 3, 19, 21
    Board of Directors of, 2, 33
    formation of, 47
Bulletins, Club, 76
Business advantage of Rotary Membership, 26, 146
Business ethics, 9, 57
Butler, R. A., 116

C

Cannock, Rotary Club of, 87, 89
Canterbury, Rotary Club of, 104, 111
Cardiff, Rotary Club of, 21
Carter, Vivian, 30, 31, 33, 34, 59, 62, 109
Central After-Care Association, the, 102
Chadwick, Arthur, 140
Charter, Club, issued by Rotary International, 17
Chatham, Rotary Club of, 89
Cheshire, Rotary in, 41
Chester, Rotary Club of, 85
Chesterfield, Rotary Club of, 85
Chesterton, G. K., 6, 148
Chicago Convention, the, 1930, 55
Chicago Headquarters of Rotary International, 17, 19, 62, 111
Chicago, Rotary Club of, 14, 151, 152
Christian names, Rotary use of, 69
Church, S. C., 84
Citizens' Advice Bureaux, 124